Shiv Puran Unlocked

A Simplified Journey

MANU SIDDHARTHA

ISBN 979-8-89744-143-3

CONTENTS

THE MAGNIFICENCE OF SHIV PURAN

VIDYESVARA SAMHITA

RUDRA SAMHITA SECTION I : CREATION

RUDRA SAMHITA SECTION II: NARRATIVE OF SATI

PREFACE

The *Shiv Puran*, one of the most revered texts within the vast ocean of Hindu scriptures, is a profound tapestry woven with intricate narratives, deep philosophical insights, and the boundless glory of Lord Shiva. It is a sacred text that has guided seekers of truth and devotees for centuries, offering a path to spiritual awakening and self-realization. However, its intricate language, complex symbolism, and the sheer volume of its verses can often present a formidable challenge, particularly for those new to Hindu philosophy or seeking a more direct understanding of its core teachings.

It is with this in mind that *Shiv Puran Unlocked: A Simplified Journey* has been lovingly crafted. This book is not intended to replace the original sacred text, nor is it a scholarly analysis meant for academics. Rather, it is an earnest attempt to bridge the gap between the profound wisdom of the *Shiva Purana* and the modern seeker. The aim is to distill its essence into language that is clear, accessible, and relatable, thereby unlocking the timeless truths it holds for all who wish to learn.

This journey through the *Shiv Puran* focuses on conveying its central themes and stories in an engaging and easy-to-understand manner. We have strived to maintain the integrity of the original text while removing the complexities that may hinder comprehension. The stories of Lord Shiva, from his cosmic dance to his divine leelas (playful acts), are presented with clarity and simplicity, inviting readers to experience the depth of his being. Similarly, the philosophical underpinnings of the text are explained in practical terms, revealing the path to self-discovery and inner peace that the *Shiv Puran* so eloquently describes.

Within these pages, you will encounter the tales of creation, the significance of devotion, the nature of karma, and the path to liberation. You will learn about the various forms of Lord Shiva and his consort, Parvati, and the rich symbolism associated with them. You will be introduced to the profound concept of the Linga and its significance in Hindu worship. You will also be presented with the stories of great sages, deities, and demons, each offering valuable lessons in the interplay between good and evil, and the importance of dharma (righteous conduct).

While this is a simplified version, every effort has been made to ensure that the true spirit and essence of the original *Shiva Purana* are preserved. This book is an invitation to embark on a journey of self-discovery through the lens of ancient wisdom. Whether you are a long-time devotee, a student of Hindu philosophy, or simply curious about the teachings of Lord Shiva, this book aims to be a gentle companion on your path.

We believe that the wisdom of the *Shiv Puran* should be accessible to all, regardless of their background or prior knowledge. This book is an offering of love, reverence, and dedication to that ideal. May the teachings of Lord Shiva, as presented here, illuminate your understanding, deepen your devotion, and bring peace and joy to your life. We hope that this book will serve as a key, unlocking the doors to a more profound connection with the divine and with your own inner self.

DEDICATION

This work, born from a deep desire to share the wisdom of the Shiv Purana in a simplified form, is offered with profound respect to my beloved Guru Maharaj, *Swami Purushottamanand Ji Maharaj*. He was more than just a teacher; he was the transformative force that awakened my own inner wisdom and set me on this path. Though he has transcended the bounds of this earthly realm, his presence remains a constant source of inspiration and guidance. His teachings continue to resonate within me, echoing in every carefully chosen word and every attempt at simplification. It is through the inner voice he nurtured that this work has come to fruition, and with a heart overflowing with gratitude, I present it as a humble offering at his lotus feet. May this effort serve as a testament to his profound impact on my life and on the lives of all those who had the privilege to know him.

About Swami Purushottamananda Ji Maharaj: The Sage of Vasishta Guha (23rd Nov 1879 - Feb. 1961)

Swami Purushottamananda Ji Maharaj, a **grand disciple of Sri Ramakrishna Paramahansa** and **disciple of Swami Brahmananda**, was a revered saint who performed intense austerities in the mystical **Vasishta Guha** since 1928. Nestled on the sacred banks of the **Ganges**, this ancient Himalayan cave has been a seat of meditation for countless sages and Siddhas. His divine presence infused the Guha with profound **spiritual**

energy, drawing seekers from around the world to experience deep meditative states and transcendental wisdom. A true beacon of devotion and enlightenment, Swami Purushottamananda Ji's legacy continues to inspire all who seek the path of inner realization.

ABOUT SHIV PURAN

The **Shiv Puran** is a sacred Hindu scripture that captures the divine conversations between **Saint Saunaka** and the **wise sage Suta**. In this discourse, Sage Suta narrates the **glory of Shiv Puran** through beautifully woven devotional stories, profound teachings, and multiple Samhitas (sections). The text serves as a spiritual guide, providing deep insights into the grandeur of **Lord Shiva** and the significance of devotion, penance, and righteous living.

Originally, the **Shiv Puran** was an expansive scripture comprising **one lakh (100,000) verses**, as narrated by **Mahadeva (Shiva) Himself**. However, recognizing the need for a more concise version suitable for the people of the Kali Yuga, **Sage Vyasa** abridged it to 24,000 verses. This act of condensation was carried out under the guidance of **Sage Sanatkumara**:

*"O sage, it is the noble Shiv Purāṇ formerly narrated by Śhiva Himself. For the benefit of the people in the age of Kali, the sage Vyasa has abridged it out of great respect for the sage **Sanatkumara** on being instructed by him."*

– Śrī Śiva Mahāpurāṇa, Mahātmya, Chapter 1

The Condensed Version by Sage Vyasa

Sage Vyasa undertook the monumental task of restructuring the Shiv Puran from its original form. Initially, the **Purāṇic lore** contained an overwhelming **one thousand million (hundred crores) verses** as conceived by Lord Shiva Himself. Over time, sages like **Dvayapayana** and others condensed it to **four hundred thousand verses**, dividing it into eighteen major Purāṇas:

"That has been condensed by Vyāsa to twenty-four thousand verses; that is to about a fourth of the original Purāṇa and he retained seven saṃhitās. The Purāṇic lore at the time of the first creation as conceived by Śiva contained a thousand million (hundred crores) verses. Dvayapayana and others condensed it into four hundred thousand verses in Dvapara and other ages which in the beginning of the Dvapara age was separated into eighteen different Purāṇas."

– Śrī Śiva Mahāpurāṇa, Vidyeśwara Saṃhitā, Chapter 2

Structure of the Shiv Puran

The **Shiv Puran** is divided into **seven distinct Samhitas**, each offering a unique aspect of **Lord Shiva's** teachings and stories. These Samhitas provide profound insights into the **three fundamental paths of devotion**:

- **Meditation (Dhyana)**

- **Prayer (Bhakti)**

- **Acts of Service (Karma)**

The **seven Samhitas** are as follows:

1. **Vidyesvara Samhita** – Discusses the supremacy of Shiva and the importance of worship.

2. **Rudra Samhita** – Chronicles the divine incarnations of Lord Shiva.

3. **Shat Rudra Samhita** – Explores the essence of Rudra and the power of his manifestations.

4. **Koti-Rudra Samhita** – Elaborates on the countless forms of Lord Shiva and their significance.

5. **Uma Samhita** – Centers around Goddess Parvati and her divine union with Lord Shiva.

6. **Kailash Samhita** – Describes the spiritual and mystical aspects of Mount Kailash, Shiva's abode.

7. **Vayaviya Samhita** – Provides esoteric knowledge and deeper philosophical insights.

This sacred scripture should be read or listened to **with deep reverence**, as it is believed to bless the devotee with wisdom, devotion, and ultimate liberation (moksha).

The Shiv Puran serves as a guiding light for those seeking a spiritual path and a deeper connection with the divine energy of Lord Shiva.

In this book, we have explained the first two Samhitas, **Vidyesvara Samhita** and **Rudra Samhita**, in a simple and easy-to-understand format for the readers, ensuring clarity and accessibility to these profound teachings.

Om Tatpurushaya Vidmahe,

Mahadevaya Dhimahi,

Tanno Rudrah Prachodayat

– Shiv Gayatri Mantra

I bow to Lord Shiva and Mata Parvati, the divine source where the whole universe surrenders; I, your humble servant, bow before You and seek Your eternal blessings for all who embark on this sacred journey through the Shiv Puran.

SHIV PURAN CHART

Shiv Puran

Samhita	Key Chronological Events	Significance
Vidyeshvara Samhita	- Creation of the universe by Shiva. - Shiva's cosmic dance (Tandava). - Dialogue between Brahma and Sanatkumara.	Introduces Shiva's supremacy, cosmic role, and the philosophy of Shaivism.
Rudra Samhita	- Shiva as Ardhanarishvara. - Shiva's Marriage with Sati - Sati's self-immolation. - Marriage of Shiva-Parvati, Kartikeya & Ganesha's birth.	Explores Shiva's dual nature (creator-destroyer), devotion, and divine love.
Shatarudra Samhita	- Destruction of Daksha's yajna (sacrifice). - Shiva as Rudra (fierce form) and Bhairava. - Teachings on rituals.	Emphasizes Shiva's wrath, cosmic justice, and rituals to appease Rudra.
Kotirudra Samhita	-Shiva's 108 names and forms. -Story of demon Andhaka's defeat. -Origin of Jyotirlingas.	Highlights Shiva's omnipresence and the power of sacred sites like Jyotirlingas.
Uma Samhita	-Parvati's penance to marry Shiva. -Dialogue on dharma, householder duties, and Shiva's teachings.	Focuses on Shakti (divine feminine) and the harmony of spiritual and worldly life.
Kailasa Samhita	- Glory of Mount Kailash. - Stories of Shiva's devotees (e.g., Ravana's encounter). - Shiva as Yogeshwara.	Symbolizes asceticism, detachment, and Shiva as the ultimate yogi.
Vayaviya Samhita	- *Purva*: Rituals, ethics, and pilgrimage. - *Uttara*: Shiva's dialogue with Skanda on moksha.	Guides worship practices and Shiva's role in liberation (moksha).

THE MAGNIFICENCE OF SHIV PURAN

Chapter One

(WHY SHIV PURAN IS SPECIAL)

The first chapter of Shiv Puran begins with a thoughtful question from Saint Saunaka to the wise sage Suta. Saunaka is eager to understand the most important teachings of the Puranas. He asks about how people can improve their behavior, deepen their devotion, and gain wisdom, especially in the challenging times of the Kali age where negative qualities seem to be increasing. He's looking for the best way to find true happiness and purity.

Sage Suta, recognizing Saunaka's sincere desire to learn, assures him that he will share the most sacred and beneficial knowledge. He introduces the **Shiv Puran** as a divine remedy that strengthens devotion to Lord Shiva and removes the great fear of death. This sacred text was originally told by Lord Shiva himself, and later summarized by the sage Vyasa for the benefit of people living in the Kali age, following instructions from the sage Sanatkumara.

The Shiv Puran is highlighted as the best way to purify the mind, particularly for people in this Kali age. It's said that only those who are intelligent and have accumulated good deeds in past lives will feel drawn to it. This sacred text is considered a form of Shiva himself and should be respected and read with complete devotion.

Reading or listening to the Shiv Puran makes a good person even more virtuous and ultimately helps them reach Shiva's divine abode. Therefore, everyone should try to read it, and listening to it with love can fulfill all desires. Simply hearing the stories of Shiva brings the same rewards as performing grand religious ceremonies.

Those who listen to the Shiv Puran are considered more than ordinary humans – they are seen as manifestations of Lord Shiva himself. The dust from the feet of those who regularly listen to and recite the Puran is considered as sacred as holy places. Anyone seeking liberation should always listen to the holy Shiv Puran with great devotion.

Even if someone can't listen to the Shiv Puran constantly, they should try to listen for a short time each day with a focused mind. If daily listening isn't possible, one should listen during holy months. Even listening for a Muhurta (48 minutes), half that period, one fourth of that period or even for a moment will not suffer from mishaps. Listening to the Puran helps one overcome the difficulties of life and eliminates the effects of negative actions.

The benefits of listening to the Shiv Puran are immense – it brings stability to the good results of charity and sacrifices. Especially in this Kali age, there's no greater way to achieve liberation than by listening to the Shiv Puran. There is no doubt that listening to the Puran and chanting Shiva's names is like a wish-fulfilling tree, granting all desires.

The Shiv Puran is like nectar that Lord Shiva has given to help those with bad thoughts and behavior in the Kali age. While ordinary nectar makes one person immortal, the nectar of Shiva's stories blesses the whole family with a kind of immortality and freedom from decay. Therefore, one should always turn to the purifying stories of the Shiv Puran.

If just listening to the Shiv Puran brings such great results, imagine the immense benefits of having Shiva residing in one's heart! This sacred text contains **24,000 verses** divided into seven sections, explaining the three paths of devotion: **meditation, prayer,** and **acts of service**. It should be listened to with deep respect. The chapter then lists the names of these seven sections. The first section is called **Vidyesvara Samhita**, the second is **Rudra Samhita**, the third is **Shat Rudra Samhita**, the fourth is **Koti-Rudra Samhita**, the fifth one is called **Uma Samhita**, the sixth one is **Kailash Samhita** and the last one is **Vayaviya Samhita**.

This divine Shiv Puran, with its seven sections, is as important as the Vedas and gives a person achievements that are greater than anything else. Someone who reads all seven sections can be considered liberated even while living. A person remains lost in the cycle of life and death until the auspicious Shiv Puran reaches their ears.

Why bother with many other scriptures that might confuse you when the Shiv Puran clearly and powerfully offers liberation? A home where the Shiv Puran is discussed becomes a holy place, destroying the sins of those who live there. The merit of thousands of horse sacrifices and hundreds of other sacrifices doesn't even equal a small part of the Shiv Puran's greatness.

A person is considered a sinner only until they hear the Shiv Puran with great devotion. The holy rivers like the Ganges, the sacred cities, and Gaya cannot compare to the power of the Shiv Puran. If someone desires the ultimate goal of liberation, they should recite at least one verse or even half a verse from the Shiv Puran. A person who constantly listens to the Shiv Puran and understands its meaning, or simply reads it with devotion, is undoubtedly a virtuous soul. Lord Shiva is very pleased with a wise person who listens to the Shiv Puran as they are nearing death and grants them a place in his own divine realm.

Someone who worships the Shiv Puran with great devotion enjoys all their desires in this world and eventually attains Shivaloka (Shiva's heaven). One should never be lazy in their devotion to the Shiv Puran. Keeping this sacred text carefully wrapped in silk will bring continuous happiness. The holy Shiv Puran is the true treasure of a Shiva devotee and should be cherished by anyone seeking happiness in this life and beyond.

The holy Shiv Puran guides people towards achieving the four main goals of life: righteousness, wealth, fulfilment of desires, and liberation. It is the greatest source of perfect well-being among the Vedas, Itihasas (epics), and other sacred texts, and those seeking liberation must understand it thoroughly. The Shiv Puran is the ultimate refuge for those seeking spiritual knowledge, the highest object of worship for good people, the remover of all kinds of suffering, the giver of lasting happiness, and it pleases all the gods, including Brahma, Vishnu, and Shiva himself.

The chapter concludes with a humble bow to the Shiv Puran, praying for continuous devotion to Lord Shiva's feet.

"Through love for Shiva, the heart finds its rest,
His holy name, from worldly ties, is blessed."

Chapter Two

(THE LIBERATION OF DEVARAJA)

This chapter starts when wise Saunaka asks Suta that who exactly gets cleaned by hearing the glorifying tale of Shiv Puran in this difficult Kalyug age. Then, Suta explains that even people who constantly sin, do bad things, or have impure thoughts can become pure by listening to the Shiv Puran. It's like a special cleansing ritual that brings both worldly happiness and spiritual freedom, pleasing Lord Shiva.

This story is focused on a man named Devaraja, a poor and ignorant Brahmin who lived in a city of Kiratas. He was dishonest, didn't worship gods, and cheated people for a living. He stole from everyone and didn't use his wealth for anything good.

One day he went to a lake to take a bath, there he saw a prostitute named Sobhavati and was much agitated at her sight. She was also much pleased to know that a rich brahmin started liking her and willing to be her slave.

The brahmin started treating her like his wife, ignoring his own family's advice. He was so seduced to her pleasant talks that even he killed his own mother, father, and first wife in his greed for their wealth.

As he was so crazy about this woman, he gave her everything he had. This included his own money and the money he had taken unfairly from his father, mother, and first wife. With this woman, who wasn't a good influence, he started eating food he shouldn't have, became addicted to alcohol, and even shared his meals from the same plate as his mistress.

One day, by chance, he came to a city of Pratisthana, there he saw a Shiva temple where some saints were assembled and narrating Shiva Purana. He stayed there and heard the discourse on Shiva. However, during his stay, he got very sick by suffering from high fever and eventually died at the end of the month.

After Devaraja's death, Yama's attendants forcefully bound him with ropes and dragged him towards Yama's city, the realm of the dead. However, this journey was abruptly interrupted by the furious arrival of Shiva's divine attendants. These celestial beings, clad in white, their bodies smeared with holy ashes, adorned with Rudraksha garlands, and brandishing tridents, descended from Sivaloka into Yama's city. They fearlessly confronted Yama's servants, overpowering them and snatching Devaraja from their grasp. Placing him in a magnificent aerial chariot, they prepared to depart for Kailasa, Shiva's heavenly abode.

The disturbance caused by this divine intervention drew the attention of Dharmaraja, the God of Death himself, who emerged from his palace to investigate. Upon seeing Shiva's four messengers, who resembled Rudra himself, Dharmaraja, recognizing their divine authority, respectfully honored them. Through his divine insight, Yama understood the situation and, filled with awe and a touch of fear, did not dare to challenge Shiva's noble attendants. After being duly venerated by Yama, Shiva's messengers proceeded to Kailasa, where they presented the redeemed Brahmin, Devaraja, to the compassionate Lord Shiva and the divine mother Parvati.

This remarkable event underscores the sanctity of the Shiv Puran, whose mere recitation possesses the power to grant salvation even to the most notorious sinners. Indeed, the supreme abode of Sadashiva is the ultimate destination, a position lauded by Vedic scholars as transcending all other realms. Even though Devaraja was a horrible person – a drunkard, obsessed with a prostitute, and the killer of his own family and many others for money – he was immediately got salvation upon arriving in Shiva's highest abode. This proves that a mere hearing of Shiv Puran, qualifies even the greatest sinner for salvation.

"Though darkest deeds may stain the soul with sin,
Shiv Puran's grace can make it pure within."

Chapter Three

(CANCULA'S DISILLUSION AND DETACHEMENT)

This chapter begins with Saunaka praising sage Suta, saying he is very smart and blessed. Saunaka says he feels very happy whenever he hears old stories, especially stories about **Shiva**. He asks Suta to tell another story that will make him even more devoted to Shiva. Saunaka believes that hearing stories about Shiva is like drinking a special drink that helps people get free from suffering and reach Shiva's heavenly abode.

Suta agrees to tell a secret story because Saunaka is a good person who knows the holy books and loves Shiva. Then, Suta begins the story of **Cancula**. It takes place in a village by the sea where most people did bad things and didn't follow good ways of living. There lived a priest named **Binduga** who was a bad man. Even though he had a good and loving wife named Cancula, he was in love with a **prostitute**. He spent all his time and money on her, even money he stole from his own parents and his first wife. He left Cancula alone.

Cancula was sad and upset at first. She tried to be a good wife, but as she got younger and stronger, she started feeling lonely and wanted a husband's love. So, she also started having a secret **lover**. One night, Binduga came home and saw Cancula with her lover. He got very angry and **hit her**. Cancula got angry back and told Binduga that he also did wrong by being with the prostitute. She said she was young and wanted love, and what else could she do since he didn't love her?

Binduga, being a bad man, told Cancula that it was okay for her to have lovers! He even told her to take money from them and give it to him, so he could use it for his prostitute. Cancula agreed to this bad idea. So, both husband and wife started living very wrong lives. After some time, Binduga

died because of his bad deeds and went to hell. He suffered a lot there and then became a **ghost** in the mountains.

Cancula continued her bad life even after Binduga died. But one day, she went to a holy place with her family. There, she heard a scholar of divine wisdom, telling stories from the **Shiv Puran**. She heard about how women who have affairs will be punished in hell. This made Cancula very scared and she started shaking.

When the narration was over, Cancula went to the wise man. She told him all the bad things she had done and felt very sorry. She said she had wasted her youth doing wrong things and was now afraid of what would happen to her after death. She asked him how she could be saved from hell.

The wise man told her not to be afraid. He said that the best way to get rid of her sins was to **love and respect Shiva** (seek refuge in Shiva) and to **feel sorry for her bad actions** (repent). He explained that hearing the stories of Shivpuran cleanses the mind, just like wiping a dirty mirror.

Cancula was very happy to hear this. She touched the wise man's feet to show her respect and promised to follow his advice. She stayed there and listened to him tell the stories of Shivpuran.

By listening to these stories, Cancula's mind became pure. She started loving Shiva with all her heart. She started dressing simply, praying, and living a good life, just like the wise man taught her.

After some time, when her life was over, Cancula died peacefully. A **divine chariot** came to take her to Shiva›s heavenly abode. She became like a goddess and saw Shiva and his wife Parvati. She was very happy and bowed to them. Because of her devotion, she got to stay in Shiva's beautiful place forever and goddess Parvati made Cancula her companion.

Later in the story, Cancula, now in Shiva's heaven, asks Parvati about her husband Binduga. Parvati tells her that he is suffering as a ghost because of his bad deeds. Cancula feels sad for him and asks Parvati how he can be saved.

Parvati, being kind, sends a divine singer named **Tumburu** to find Binduga's ghost. Tumburu forces the ghost to listen to the entire Shivpuran.

Just like it helped Cancula, hearing the holy stories cleanses Binduga's soul. He is freed from being a ghost, gets a divine body, and is finally reunited with Cancula in Shiva's heaven. This emphasizes that even those who have done great wrong can be saved and obtain liberation through the power of listening Shiv Puran with complete devotion.

"Listening Shiv Puran, can make good prevail,
From sinful ears heard, no longer to fail."

Chapter Four

(THE RULES FOR LISTENING TO SHIV PURAN)

In this chapter, we delve into the proper way to listen to the stories of the *Shiv Puran*, ensuring we receive the full blessings they offer. The wise sage Saunaka, eager to understand the art of sacred listening, asks the learned Suta how one should approach these divine narratives. Suta explains that to gain the most from the *Shiv Puran*, the process must begin with careful preparation.

First, *the planning of the discourse must be meticulous*. The organizer of the listening – often a householder – should consult an astrologer to find an auspicious day to begin, ensuring that nothing will interrupt the telling. Then, invitations must be sent far and wide, welcoming not only the devout but also women, those from lower social standings, and anyone who may not usually participate in such sacred gatherings. These invitations should be extended with humility and warmth, welcoming all, even those who can only stay for a short while.

The place for the storytelling must also be carefully selected, choosing a clean and holy spot like a Shiva temple, a sacred place, a park, or even a home. The space should be made beautiful with decorations, and a high platform should be prepared for the storyteller, accompanied by comfortable seating for the listeners. The overall atmosphere should be one of joy, mirroring the excitement of a wedding, free from any earthly concerns.

During the discourse itself, the storyteller should face north or east, as would a worshipper, or directly face the audience. While narrating, they should not bow to anyone, highlighting their elevated role. ***The status and role of the storyteller is paramount.*** Listeners should view the storyteller as a sacred

teacher, even more precious than any worldly instructor, deserving of the utmost respect. The storyteller, a person of virtue, skill, and eloquence, should begin at sunrise and continue for approximately seven and a half hours.

The sacred stories should not be told to bad or argumentative people, nor in places where ill-reputed individuals gather. The storyteller should take breaks for personal needs but otherwise maintain focus on their sacred duty. They should also have a learned assistant nearby to address any questions or concerns from the listeners. Before the discourse begins, prayers should be offered to Ganesha, Shiva, and the *Shiv Puran* book, to remove any obstacles from the storytelling.

The preparation of the mind and heart of the listeners is equally important as the physical preparations. Listeners should approach the words with reverence, focus, and understanding, purifying their minds and opening their hearts to divine wisdom. They should refrain from worldly distractions and listen with an unwavering faith. Those who do not follow these rules, allowing their minds to wander to lust, anger, or earthly matters, will receive little benefit.

Moreover, listeners should avoid certain behaviors, for they are seen as disrespectful. Leaving mid-discourse, covering one's head with a turban, chewing betel leaves, sitting on a higher seat, adopting a particular yoga pose, failing to bow to the storyteller, lying down (unless ill), sitting at the same level as the speaker, speaking ill of the storyteller or the stories, arguing, or refusing to listen will lead to negative outcomes. Instead, ***the ideal listener is characterized by purity, devotion, and attentiveness.***

Each day should conclude with worship of Ganesha, the nine planets, the deities and an offering of humble prayers to the *Shivpurana* itself, acknowledging it as one with Shiva, to have the ability to conclude the discourse without obstacle. The organizers must also honor the storyteller with gifts and offerings and maintain a solemn promise of devotion. In this way, one seeks to gain true wisdom and understanding through the sacred stories. They should invite knowledgeable men to chant the Shiva Panchakshara mantra, adding blessings to the occasion.

In conclusion, Suta shares with Saunaka these sacred guidelines for listening to the *Shiv Puran*, ensuring that all who follow them will receive the greatest benefit.

"Let Shivpuran's flow, make your spirit pure and light,
And guide your steps on path that's good and right."

(DO'S AND DONT'S OF LISTENING TO SHIV PURAN)

Saunaka, recognizing Suta's deep devotion and understanding of the Shiv Puran, initiates a vital inquiry. He implores Suta, *"Oh Suta, foremost among devotees of Shiva, you have narrated this wonderfully auspicious story. Please, for the benefit of the whole world, tell me the rules governing those who perform the rite of listening to Shiv Puran."* This pivotal question sets the stage for a detailed exploration of the practices and principles that underpin a truly transformative listening experience.

Suta, acknowledging the importance of Saunaka's inquiry, proceeds to explain the essential guidelines for those who aspire to listen to the Shiv Puran with reverence. "Oh Saunaka," he begins, *"Listen with devotion to the rules governing those persons. If you hear the excellent story with due observance of the rules, the fruit is excellent and there is no obstacle in the achievement of the fruit."* This statement underscores the core principle: that listening to these sacred narratives is not a passive activity but a spiritual practice requiring intention, discipline, and adherence to a structured approach. Suta emphasizes that these rules are not restrictive but are designed to ensure the listener can fully benefit from the profound wisdom contained within the Shiv Puran.

Preparing the Body and Mind: The Foundation for Sacred Listening

Before embarking on the path of listening to the Shiv Puran, several preparatory steps are necessary. The listener should ideally undergo initiation, signifying a commitment to the path of learning and spiritual growth. During the period of listening, a disciplined daily routine is encouraged. This includes a single meal at the end of each day's session, preferably eaten from a leaf plate, a practice symbolic of simplicity. Purity during this period is also advised, to help channel all energies towards spiritual absorption. Moreover, the body's rest should be humble, with sleep on the ground instead of a bed, to further detach the mind from worldly comfort. Fasting is considered beneficial for those with the capacity, with options ranging from a complete fast to a diet of milk, ghee, or fruit, or a single, simple meal. It is not about causing hardship to the body, but about having

a balanced diet, while keeping the mind focused on listening. The guiding principle is to maintain a physical state that supports mental clarity and spiritual receptivity. The dietary restrictions are very specific; very heavy, difficult to digest foods, certain vegetables and strong spices should be avoided, as these are believed to interfere with the mind's receptiveness.

Cultivating Inner Purity: The Ethical Code for Listening

The preparation for listening extends beyond physical discipline into the realm of inner purity. The listener is called upon to actively avoid negative emotions such as lust, anger, and hatred. Disrespect towards any group, or those following a pure and virtuous life is strictly prohibited. The avoidance of negative influences extends to social interactions as well, the listener should avoid looking at women in their menstrual cycle and should keep away from engaging in conversation with those with negative qualities or disbelief in ancient scriptures. These guidelines are designed to create a space of inner harmony and peacefulness. Instead of harboring such negativity, listeners are encouraged to cultivate virtues such as honesty, cleanliness, compassion, humility, and truthfulness. This cultivation of positive qualities makes the mind more open to the sacred truths within the Shiv Puran.

Benefits of Listening: Rewards of Devotion and Discipline

The text outlines the manifold benefits that arise from listening to the Shiv Puran with the proper devotion and adherence to guidelines. The listener can approach the teachings with a specific goal or desire, with the assurance that their intentions will be fulfilled. This listening process can also be without any expectation or desire for any material gain, and instead, with the aim to achieve salvation, a state of freedom from the cycle of birth and death. This process is not just about the individual listener but is also beneficial for all people in any situation.

The time dedicated to listening is considered to be sacred, equivalent to many great sacrifices. The act of giving, even small gifts, during these listening sessions, is said to produce significant and long lasting positive outcomes.

The Completion of Listening: Rituals and Offerings

The conclusion of the listening session is marked by specific rituals and practices. An optional celebratory ceremony, known as "Udyapana," akin to a graduation, is advised to complete the event and can be conducted by those who have the capacity. The book of the Shiv Puran itself is revered through worship, treated with the same respect as one would give to the deity Shiva. The presentation of gifts such as new cloth and strings, or other material gifts to those who have taken their time to narrate the story is an offering that will help them with their future lives. Following the listening session, it is recommended to host gatherings with food, music and dance, to continue sharing the wisdom and positivity gained. Further contemplation through the recitation or listening to other ancient scriptures and the performance of the fire ritual called 'homa' is also recommended to purify the ritual and remove any defects. There should also be chanting of the thousand names of Shiva, which helps to remove any imperfections in the listening process. Finally, it's recommended to offer food to eleven Brahmins. With all of these rituals and offerings, if you have the capacity to do so, and you have followed the path with complete devotion, it is believed that you will receive the grace of Shiva and attain liberation.

The Essence of the Shiv Puran: A Path to Liberation

The chapter concludes by highlighting the significance of the Shiv Puran as a pivotal text for spiritual seekers. It is considered the most significant of the Puranas, and by engaging with it devotedly, one can begin to alleviate the sufferings of life and finally reach ultimate salvation. The text reiterates that those who meditate on, speak of, and listen to the stories of Shiva will ultimately transcend the cycle of birth and death. It is an invitation to seek refuge in the infinite bliss of Shiva, a being whose essence is beyond human understanding, yet accessible through devotion.

"Through pure devotion, hearts align,
Listening transforms the soul divine."

VIDYESVARA SAMHITA

Chapter One

(THE SAGES' DILEMMA: A WORLD GRIPPED BY KALI YUGA)

The Vidyesvara Samhita, the first book of the Shiva Purana, begins not with a divine act, but with a very human concern: the suffering of humanity. This chapter sets the stage for the entire Purana, revealing the dire circumstances that necessitate the intervention of divine wisdom. We start with a moment of reverence, an invocation to Lord Shiva. This powerful prayer acknowledges Shiva as the source of all auspiciousness, the master of the self, eternal and the remover of all sins.

The scene then shifts to a more earthly setting - Prayag, the sacred confluence of the Ganga and Yamuna rivers. Here, a group of spiritually enlightened sages are engaged in a grand sacrifice, their hearts filled with devotion and their minds focused on the higher truths. These sages, deeply committed to righteous conduct, are the custodians of ancient wisdom and are disturbed by the growing darkness they witness in the world. Their actions signify a deep yearning for spiritual upliftment.

Into this sacred space, arrives Suta, a revered scholar of the Puranas and the dedicated disciple of Vyasa. He is greeted with the utmost respect by the sages, who acknowledge his vast knowledge and wisdom. Suta's arrival is a beacon of hope to the assembled sages. They recognize him as the repository of ancient stories and teachings, believing him to be the key to understanding and addressing the turmoil they observe in the world. The sages' humble welcome highlights the importance of knowledge and respect in the quest for truth.

The sages, after extending warm hospitality to Suta, voice their deep concern over the deteriorating state of the world in the current age of Kali Yuga. They express their anguish at the moral and spiritual decay they witness everywhere, describing the world with a bleak picture of humanity. They tell Suta about the widespread abandonment of dharma (righteous conduct), and the rise of selfishness, greed, and moral turpitude. They vividly describe how people have fallen prey to materialism, lost respect for their elders and parents, and become obsessed with sensual gratification. The Brahmins are now selling the knowledge of Vedas, the Kshatriyas are cowards, and the Vaishyas have lost their honesty. These are not just individual acts of wrongdoings, but rather the breakdown of the entire societal structure. The visual representation emphasizes the gravity of their concerns and helps connect with the reader on an emotional level.

Furthermore, the sages reveal that women have abandoned their duties and fidelity, and children are growing up without any moral compass. The traditional social classes – Brahmins, Kshatriyas, Vaishyas, and Shudras – have all deviated from their respective paths, resulting in societal chaos and spiritual decline. They lament that the purpose of life seems to be lost, with people focusing on fleeting pleasures and selfish desires. This breakdown of moral and social structures makes salvation for the people extremely difficult.

In their despair, the sages turn to Suta, seeking his guidance. They believe that he, being the embodiment of the Puranic wisdom, holds the key to their salvation. They implore him to reveal the easiest and most effective remedy for the collective sins of humanity, a path that will lead them to spiritual liberation. Suta, realizing the urgency of their plea, then remembers Lord Shiva before he begins to address the troubled sages, marking the start of the profound teachings to come.

Chapter Two

(ANSWERS CLARIFYING THE DOUBTS OF THE SAGES)

The second chapter begins with Suta, the wise narrator, addressing the assembly of troubled sages with compassion and understanding. He acknowledges their pressing concerns about the state of the world, assuring them that he will share the knowledge that can liberate people from the darkness of Kali Yuga. Suta begins by emphasizing the immense significance of the Shiva Purana. He declares that this sacred text embodies the very essence of Vedanta – the core philosophy of the Vedas. Suta explains that the Shiva Purana is more than just a collection of stories; it's a divine guide that can destroy sins, lead to enlightenment, and ultimately bring about liberation (Moksha).

Suta continues, highlighting the exceptional power of the Shiva Purana, calling it a powerful force that dispels the negative influences of Kali Yuga. He explains that it reveals the glorious nature of Lord Shiva, capable of granting the four aims of human life: Dharma (righteous conduct), Artha (prosperity), Kama (desire), and Moksha (liberation). He emphasizes that a sincere study of the Shiva Purana will pave the way for salvation. He uses vivid language and imagery, saying that the Shiva Purana has not yet risen high, that is, as long as its message hasn't been widely received, the sins, disputes, and miseries of Kali Yuga will continue.

Suta explains how, until the Shiva Purana's teachings are prevalent, negativity and disputes are rampant. The text describes a world where the sacred scriptures themselves clash, where even holy sites and mantras are engaged in bitter disagreements. He mentions how Yama's (god of death) cruel attendants roam fearlessly because of the absence of Shiva Purana in people's life. He highlights the supremacy of the Shiva Purana over other

Puranas, claiming that until the Shiva Purana has risen, other Puranas roar loudly. He further states that even understanding Lord Shiva's divine nature is difficult without the wisdom contained in this sacred text.

Moving beyond the theoretical importance, Suta begins to describe the practical benefits of engaging with the Shiva Purana. He explains that even reading a single verse or half a verse with devotion is enough to destroy sins. He calls anyone who studies the Shiva Purana daily and with alertness a **"Jivanmukta"** – a liberated soul even while living. He equates reading or worshipping the Shiva Purana with the performance of the horse-sacrifice, a very potent ritual. Suta also emphasizes that just listening to the Shiva Purana, even from someone who is not as great as him, will free people from their sins.

Suta then describes a number of actions one can take, such as copying the Shiva Purana and offering it to devotees, which is equal to the merit of studying all scriptures. He highlights specific rituals like fasting on the Chaturdasi (fourteenth day of the lunar fortnight) and engaging in discourses on the Shiva Purana, leading to great spiritual merit, equivalent to chanting the Gayatri mantra. He further explains the power of reciting the Shiva Purana during a night vigil on Chaturdasi. He also talks about the merits achieved from reciting specific parts of Shiva Purana, such as Rudra Samhita.

Suta then explains the original size and structure of the Shiva Purana, revealing that it was initially comprised of 100,000 verses divided into twelve Samhitas (sections). However, Sage Vyasa condensed it to 24,000 verses across seven Samhitas, making it more accessible to people. He lists the names of the seven Samhitas: Vidyesvara, Rudra, Satarudra, Kotirudra, Uma, Kailasa and Vayaviya. Suta highlights that the Shiva Purana, in its condensed form, is equivalent to the Vedas and grants liberation. He finally concludes by stressing that the Shiva Purana, which was first revealed by Shiva himself and later compiled by Vyasa, is the ultimate text for spiritual liberation, offering pure and true wisdom.

Chapter Three

(THE DELIBERATION ON THE ACHIEVABLE AND THE MEANS OF ACHIEVEMENT)

This chapter delves into the core teachings of the Shiva Purana, focusing on how to connect with Lord Shiva and achieve liberation. It begins with the sages, still eager to learn more, requesting Suta to narrate the essence of Vedanta, the ultimate knowledge. Suta, pleased with their eagerness, first meditates on Shiva.

Then he begins to narrate the divine wisdom. He emphasizes that the Shiva Purana is the supreme text that blends devotion, wisdom, and non-attachment. He stresses that it reveals the ultimate truth, which can only be realized through the study of Vedanta.

The chapter then describes a time in the distant past when a great dispute arose among sages from six different groups, each holding their own views on who is supreme.

These sages approached Lord Brahma, the creator, for guidance. They asked him about the imperishable and the greatest being. Brahma, in response, reveals the supremacy of Lord Mahadeva (Shiva), stating that Shiva is beyond comprehension by the mind and senses and that He is the ultimate source from which everything—including Brahma, Vishnu, Rudra, and all the elements—has emerged. Brahma explains that devotion to Shiva, achieved through His grace, is the only way to know him. He also adds that devotion comes from the grace of Shiva and his grace is the result of devotion, just like how seed produces sprout and sprout produces the seed.

Brahma instructs the sages to descend to earth and perform a thousand-year-long sacrifice to propitiate Lord Shiva. He tells them that through Shiva's grace, they will realize the path to achieving their highest goal. The sages then ask Brahma about the nature of that goal and the means to reach it. Brahma explains that the ultimate goal is to reach Shiva's realm, which can be attained through devotion and service to Him. The true seeker is free from all desires, and this detachment is also a gift from Shiva. Actions performed according to the Vedas, with their fruits dedicated to Shiva, can lead to *Salokya* – attaining residence in the same world as Shiva. Brahma reveals that devotion is key, and it comes in many forms as revealed by Ishvara himself.

Finally, Brahma condenses the path to achieving Shiva into three main steps: listening to Shiva's glory (*Shravana*), praising Shiva with words (*Kirtana*), and deeply contemplating Shiva in the mind (*Manana*). He stresses that *Shravana* is the most important first step, which involves listening to the teachings from a teacher. Following this, one must practice *Kirtana* and *Manana*. By consistently practicing these steps, one can gradually attain Shiva Yoga – unification with Shiva – and experience supreme bliss, free from all suffering. Brahma explains that while the initial process might be difficult, it leads to a state of eternal auspiciousness.

Chapter Four

(THE POWER OF LISTENING, PRAISING, AND THINKING ABOUT SHIVA)

This chapter is all about how we can connect with Lord Shiva and find peace and freedom. The sages ask Brahma, "What exactly are Shravana, Kirtana, and Manana?" They want to understand these three steps to liberation in detail.

Brahma explains that the mind naturally likes to think and analyze. *Manana,* which means deep contemplation, is like using your mind to explore and understand Shiva's qualities, His stories, and His different names. It's like trying to understand why you love someone so much — you keep thinking about them. Brahma says that this ability to ponder and delve deeper into Shiva is a gift from Shiva himself. He stresses that this constant act of thinking about Shiva is the most vital of all the paths to him.

Kirtana is all about expressing your love for Shiva. It could be through singing devotional songs, reciting stories about him, or even just speaking about him in your own words. This singing or speaking can be done in any language and is another important step to connect with Shiva. This is the middle of the three paths.

Shravana means listening to anything about Shiva with a focused and loving mind, whether it›s a story, a teaching, or even just hearing someone talk about Him. It's like listening to a loved one telling you a story of how they achieved success. The more you listen with a calm and attentive heart, the closer you get to Shiva. It's like a lover listening to all the stories and talks of his beloved. It becomes more easier as one associates with good people who are already on their path. Brahma says that all three — Shravana, Kirtana, and Manana, are gifts from Shiva's grace.

To explain further, Suta tells a story about his teacher, Vyasa, who was feeling lost despite being a wise sage. Vyasa was doing penance by the bank of the Saraswati river, and felt agitated. Sanatkumara, another wise sage, saw Vyasa. Sanatkumara told him that Lord Shiva can be realized by thinking about him. He then told Vyasa that *Shravana, Kirtana,* and *Manana* are the right paths to reach salvation.

Sanatkumara explained that he himself had performed many penances on Mount Mandara but found clarity when Shiva's attendant, Nandikeshvara, advised him on these three steps. Therefore, Vyasa too was advised to practice *Shravana, Kirtana,* and *Manana.* Then Sanatkumara returned to his divine abode.

Chapter Five

(THE SPECIAL MEANING OF SHIVA'S LINGAM)

This chapter explains why Lord Shiva is worshipped not just in a human-like form, but also as a *lingam* (a phallic symbol). The chapter begins by saying that if someone is unable to follow the paths of *Shravana* (listening), *Kirtana* (praising), and *Manana* (thinking), as mentioned in the last chapter, they can worship a *lingam* or an image of Shiva daily. It's like having a personal symbol to focus on for your devotion. This act of worship, along with offering gifts as one can afford, can help them overcome the difficulties of life. It›s like a simple but effective way to connect with the divine.

The chapter goes on to explain how this worship should be performed with devotion, elaborate decorations and offering as one can afford. All of these acts are done with great reverence and intention. This worship, whether elaborate or simple, is said to bring liberation. Many people have achieved salvation through this worship.

Then, the sages ask a very important question: "Why is Shiva worshipped both as an image and as a lingam, while other gods are only worshipped as images?"

Suta, the narrator, explains that this question is special because Shiva himself revealed the answer. Shiva has two aspects: *Niskala* and *Sakala*. *Niskala* means formless and beyond description, like the energy that exists everywhere. *Sakala* means with form, like his familiar human-like representation. The *lingam* represents Shiva›s *Niskala* aspect, his formless, supreme reality. When one worships an idol they are worshipping his *Sakala* aspect i.e. with form.

Suta says that because Shiva is both *Niskala* and *Sakala*, he can be worshipped in both forms. Other gods, who are not the supreme Brahman, only have a *Sakala* aspect; so they are worshipped only in their images. It's similar to how we have a name and form in the world, but deep within we are an infinite consciousness. Shiva embodies both. This explanation comes from the teachings of Nandikeshvara to Sanatkumara on Mount Mandara, while discussing the meaning of the sacred syllable Om.

Sanatkumara then asks Nandikeshvara, "Why does Shiva have this lingam form, while others don't?"

Nandikeshvara explains that the *lingam* is a symbol of Shiva›s unmanifested form. In the first *Kalpa* (a cosmic cycle), Brahma and Vishnu started fighting over who was superior. To end their arrogance, Lord Shiva appeared as a column of light without form. Then, from this column, the *lingam* emerged, as a blessing to all worlds. It's like a special gift of grace to the world.

So, from that time, the *lingam* and the image are both used to worship Shiva. Other gods are worshipped in their images to grant people certain pleasures and enjoyments. However, Shiva is worshipped in both forms for enjoyment as well as salvation. Therefore, worship of Lingam or Image of Shiva can be done according to devotee›s preferences.

Chapter Six

(WHEN GODS FIGHT AND SEEK REFUGE WITH SHIVA)

This chapter tells a story of a big fight between Lord Brahma and Lord Vishnu, and how the other gods seek shelter with Lord Shiva. It all begins with Vishnu resting on his serpent couch, with the goddess of fortune and his attendants nearby. Just then, Brahma arrives.

Brahma, proud and thinking he is superior, questions Vishnu, who is lying down and not paying attention to his arrival. He demands that Vishnu acknowledge him as his Lord. Vishnu calmly welcomes Brahma and asks him to sit down. Brahma then declares himself to be the protector of the world, and Vishnu's father. Vishnu angrily replies that the whole universe is within him, and he is the one who created Brahma from his navel.

Both the gods, each believing they were superior, start arguing and get ready to fight, like two stubborn goats. They begin to battle using their divine powers. Brahma rides a swan and Vishnu rides a Garuda. The attendants of both the deities also got into a clash.

Other gods in their chariots come to watch the big fight. Vishnu gets very angry and shoots powerful weapons at Brahma, and Brahma responds in the same way by shooting fiery arrows. The fight becomes very intense. Vishnu then uses the *Maheshvara* weapon, and Brahma retaliates with the *Pashupata* weapon. These are incredibly powerful weapons that clash with each other in the sky, creating a terrifying scene of roaring wind. The whole scene was filled with terrifying weapons flying everywhere.

The other gods, witnessing this fight, become frightened and helpless. They know that Lord Shiva is the supreme God who is the creator, preserver, and destroyer. They also realize that without his will, not even a blade of grass can move. Therefore, they decide to go to Shiva's abode on Mount Kailash and seek his protection.

They bow their heads in reverence as they reach Kailash and enter Shiva's palace. There, they see Shiva sitting on a gem-studded seat, with Uma (Parvati) by his side. He is sitting with his right leg over the left knee, his hands resting on his legs, and attendants are all around him. The Vedas are being chanted, and Shiva is blessing everyone.

Seeing Shiva, the gods' eyes fill with joy. They kneel from afar, and Shiva, pleased to see them, asks his attendants to bring the gods closer. With a calm and compassionate voice, Shiva addresses them.

Chapter Seven

(SHIVA'S DIVINE INTERVENTION)

This chapter tells the story of a massive conflict and the dramatic way Lord Shiva intervenes to restore balance. The chapter opens with Shiva, the supreme being, addressing the gods, assuring them that all is well with the universe and their duties. However, he acknowledges that he is aware of the ongoing fight between Lord Brahma and Lord Vishnu. He gently dismisses their worries, telling them their concerns are like unnecessary chatter, and assures them that he knows the way to solve this dispute. Shiva then announces his intention to personally visit the battlefield where Brahma and Vishnu are warring.

He assembles his army of attendants and commands a hundred of his commanders to prepare for the journey. The air fills with the sound of different musical instruments, signaling the start of their procession.

Shiva mounts his special chariot, shaped like the sacred sound "Om," adorned with five circular rings. He is accompanied by his sons, his Ganas (attendants), and all the other gods, including Indra.

The procession is a grand spectacle, marked by colorful banners, the waving of fans, the scattering of flowers, and the enchanting sounds of music and dance. Along with the great goddess Parvati, Pasupati (another name for Shiva) travels towards the battlefield. However, upon reaching the battlefield, Lord Shiva suddenly vanishes, and the music, as well as the commotion of his attendants and army, falls silent.

On the battlefield, Brahma and Vishnu are consumed by their fight, hurling deadly weapons at each other, each believing he is the ultimate power. The flames from their weapons start to threaten the entire universe. It becomes clear that the three worlds are on the brink of destruction. Seeing this, Lord Shiva takes a form unlike any other to stop this impending devastation: He appears as a gigantic, towering column of fire! This enormous column of fire is so vast and intense that the weapons of Brahma and Vishnu are immediately drawn into it, effectively ending the battle and preventing the destruction of the universe.

Stunned by this amazing phenomenon, Brahma and Vishnu are both confused and curious, wondering what this colossal fire column could possibly be. They decide to explore it, setting out to find both the top and bottom of this unfathomable form. However, both of them decide to go their own ways, as they thought they may achieve less if they go together. Vishnu transforms himself into a boar, digging down through the earth in search of the root of the fiery column. Brahma, on the other hand, takes the form of a swan and flies upwards, attempting to find the top.

Despite their best efforts, both Brahma and Vishnu fail in their quests. Vishnu, after digging through the netherworlds, returns exhausted, unable to find the base of the column. Brahma, while flying upwards, encounters a Ketaki flower falling from the middle of the fiery column. The flower tells Brahma that it has been falling a very long time and has not found the top of the column. Brahma, realizing he too cannot reach the top, asks the Ketaki flower to lie and tell Vishnu that it witnessed Brahma reach the top. The Ketaki flower agrees to lie.

Brahma returns to the battlefield, where he meets Vishnu. Vishnu, being truthful, admits that he couldn't find the base. Brahma, however, falsely claims to have reached the top of the fiery column, with the Ketaki flower confirming his lie. Vishnu, thinking this to be true, then honors and respects Brahma. Finally, Lord Shiva appears in his usual form from the fiery column, revealing Brahma's deceit. Vishnu, full of remorse, begs for forgiveness. Shiva then praises Vishnu's honesty, stating that because he upheld the truth despite his ambition, he will be equally honored and respected like himself. Shiva declares that they will have separate temples and forms of worship.

This chapter concludes with Shiva establishing the equal status of Vishnu, rewarding his truthfulness, and laying the foundation for separate worship practices for both gods, witnessed by all the other Gods.

Chapter Eight

(SHIVA'S FORGIVENESS OF BRAHMA)

This chapter tells us a story about how Lord Shiva taught Brahma a lesson in humility. Brahma, one of the main gods, had become arrogant. To deal with this, Lord Shiva created a powerful being named Bhairava from the middle of his own eyebrows. Bhairava, looking like a fierce warrior, kneeled before Lord Shiva, asking for instructions. Lord Shiva told Bhairava to punish Brahma because he had spoken a lie and also behaved proudly.

Bhairava, following Lord Shiva's orders, grabbed Brahma by his fifth head (which was the one that told the lie). Bhairava raised his sword to chop off that head. Brahma, scared to death, fell at Bhairava's feet, trembling like a weak tree. His ornaments scattered and he looked utterly defeated. Vishnu, seeing Brahma's plight, pleaded with Shiva to forgive him.

Lord Shiva, moved by Vishnu's request, stopped Bhairava. He then scolded Brahma for trying to act like the supreme lord to gain respect. Lord Shiva decreed that Brahma wouldn't be honored or have his own temples or festivals. This was a huge punishment for a god! Brahma then asked Lord Shiva to forgive him, saying even being spared was a big blessing. Lord Shiva, acknowledging that the universe needs a structure, told Brahma he will punish the guilty and rule justly and further stated that Brahma would be essential for all sacrifices. He added that all ceremonies performed without Brahma's presence would be useless.

Finally, Shiva also punished a Ketaki flower. This flower had lied for Brahma. Shiva banished it from his worship. The flower begged forgiveness and asked to be made meaningful. So, Shiva said that while he wouldn't wear it, his followers could, and it could be used in decorations. In this way even the Ketaki flower was given a purpose. Shiva finally blessed the three: Ketaki, Brahma and Vishnu and shined in the assembly being praised by all the Gods.

This chapter shows that even great beings can make mistakes and that humility is very important. Shiva is portrayed as fair, understanding and compassionate, willing to forgive but also to teach valuable lessons.

Chapter Nine

(SHIVA IS DECLARED THE SUPREME LORD (MAHESHWARA))

This chapter describes how Lord Shiva established his supreme authority after appearing as a massive pillar of fire. Brahma and Vishnu, awestruck, respectfully worshipped him with precious items. Pleased with their devotion, Shiva declared that this day would be known as "**Shivaratri**", and that anyone who worships, the Lingam, or an image of him on this day would receive great merit and the ability to create, protect and destroy the world.

Lord Shiva also explained that Shivaratri must be observed with fasting, sincerity and control of senses. He then revealed that he appeared as the pillar of fire on the day of the Ardra star in the month of **Margasirsa**, and that seeing him with Parvati and worshipping the Lingam on this day is extremely auspicious. This site was named "**Lingasthana**", and for the sake of worship the fiery column would become smaller as the Linga.

Shiva explained that the Lingam is a source of both worldly joy and salvation and that just seeing, touching, or thinking about the Lingam can free one from the cycle of birth and death. The place where this all happened would now be known as "**Aruna Mountain**", and any death or living on the sacred site guarantees liberation. He stressed that this is the most sacred place and that remembrance there grants salvation.

Lord Shiva declared that he has two forms: the manifest form and the unmanifest form and no one else has these two forms, making them 'non-Ishvara'. He declared that he appeared in front of them as a pillar, symbolizing his formless essence, and in his current form, representing his role as the Lord. He stressed that both these forms are exclusive to him alone and none other, even Brahma and Vishnu could claim to be the Ishvara. He said that their ignorance and ego caused the fight, and therefore, he had to appear before them. Lord Shiva asked them to give up their ego and recognize him as the supreme lord. He ended by saying that he is the supreme Brahman because of his vastness and the fact that he causes everything to grow. He is the Atman due to his equal nature and his pervasiveness. He declared that all others are Anatma and he is the only one who carries out creation, destruction, and liberation of the universe. He clarified that his fiery column is a symbol of his Brahman form, and this current form is his Ishvara manifestation. He told them that the Linga is the symbol of his Brahman essence and must be worshipped.

Lord Shiva then explained the importance of the Lingam, stating that it is his symbol and that it should be worshipped as himself. He clarified that the Lingam represents his formless essence, and by installing it one is essentially installing him. Installing the Lingam leads to union with Shiva. He stated that installing the Lingam is primary and installing his statue is secondary.

Chapter Ten

(THE FIVE DUTIES OF SHIVA AND THE POWER OF OM)

In this chapter, Brahma and Vishnu ask Lord Shiva to explain his five main duties, what they are and how they are performed. Lord Shiva explained these duties are the cycle of existence: creation, maintenance, destruction, concealment, and liberation. Creation is bringing the universe into being, maintenance is sustaining it, destruction is its end, concealment is temporary removal for renewal and liberation is freedom from the cycle. Shiva said that these are all his powers and he uses other forces to enact these, but liberation is his sole privilege. He also connected each duty to the five elements: earth (creation), water (maintenance), fire (destruction), wind (concealment), and sky (liberation). He said that he has five faces to perform these duties, and that Brahma and Vishnu were given the first two duties but Rudra and Mahesh got the next two. He emphasized that the final power of liberation rests with him alone. Lord Shiva also explains that Brahma and Vishnu forgot these truths due to lack of meditation and thus had the illusion of being supreme.

To help them, Lord Shiva shared the sacred mantra "Om," revealing that it came from him and is one with him. He said that repeating "Om" is like remembering him. The different sounds within "Om" originate from his five faces and represent both Shiva and Shakti, the masculine and feminine powers of the universe. He stated that the mantra 'Namah Shivaya' is also a form of him. From this, the five mothers and 'Siromantra' was born. He also added that all the Vedas and many other mantras originated from him, but that "Om" is the most fundamental and can achieve everything. Along with his consort Ambika, Lord Shiva took Brahma and Vishnu as his disciples, placed his hands on their heads and taught them the "Om" mantra and its rituals. They then gave themselves to Lord Shiva and offered prayers.

Lord Shiva instructed them to recite the mantra with the guidance of Goddess, saying it will give them wisdom and prosperity, especially when repeated on special days. He emphasized that though his Linga and statue are both important, Linga is better for worship. He told them that Linga is to be installed with the "Om" mantra while statues are to be installed with the five-syllable mantra, enabling one to easily reach him. He then disappeared after giving these teachings. This chapter emphasizes the power of "Om" and the path of devotion to connect with the divine.

Chapter Eleven

(HOW TO WORSHIP SHIVA'S LINGAM AND OFFERINGS)

This chapter begins with the sages asking Suta about the proper way to worship Lord Shiva's Lingam. They want to know about its characteristics, the right time and place for worship, and who is qualified to perform it. Suta explains that the *time* for worship should be convenient and auspicious, and the *place* should be a holy center, like a river bank, or anywhere that allows for daily worship. The Lingam can be made of earth, water, or fire type materials. A Lingam made with all the characteristics laid out in sacred texts, gives great rewards. A subtle, smaller Lingam is good for mobile worship, while a larger, gross one is suitable for stationary worship. The Lingam should have a seat that matches its nature like circular, square or triangular shapes. However, the best seat is like a cot. In the beginning Lingams were made of earth and stone but later made of metal as well. If a Lingam is stationary both the emblem and its base should be of the same material. But if mobile then the base and Lingam can be different except for the one worshipped by Asura Bana.

The height of the Lingam should be about 12 finger-widths of the person worshipping. Shorter Lingams are not as effective, but longer ones are fine. A slight difference in size for mobile Lingams is acceptable. A beautifully decorated "Vimana," a chariot-like structure, with divine attendants should be made. The sanctum should have the nine precious gems and the Lingam should be installed on an altar. The Lingam should be worshipped with mantras like "Sadyo" etc. in five places along with fire offerings. Lord Shiva and his family should be worshipped and the priest must be gifted. Money should also be given to the poor and all living beings should be treated with respect. The cavity on which the Lingam rests should be filled with precious gems. All the mantras should be recited, and the Lingam and its base should be united together with love and devotion. The embodied images are installed outside the main sanctum for festivals using the five-syllable mantra.

Suta then explains that there are two types of Lingams: stationary (like trees) and mobile (like insects). For stationary Lingams, care and upkeep is important; for mobile ones, offering of water is key. He says that the Lingam represents the sentient being and the base (Pitha) represents Parvati, Shiva's consort. And just as Shiva is ever-embraced by Parvati, the Lingam always remains connected to the Pitha. This is the essence of the installation of the Lingam. He also explains that daily worship should be performed according to one's capacity and banners should also be installed. Worshipping a mobile Lingam with 16 different kinds of service, yields similar results, and these include invitation, offering of seat, water, washing feet, mouth rinse, oil bath, cloth, scents, flowers, incense, lamps, food, lights, betel leaves, respect, and concluding with immersion. Alternatively, one can do only the water offering to food offering part of the ceremony or just the basic rites, such as bath, food offerings and obeisance. Worshipping Lingam as described in the above manner leads to region of Shiva. All these rites can be performed on any Lingam, whether it is made by humans, saints, gods, or is self-born or extraordinary in nature.

Gifting items used in worship will yield benefits. Regular visits to the Linga and performing circumambulation and obeisance will slowly lead to Shiva's abode. Even creating a Linga from clay, cow dung, flowers, jaggery, butter, ash, or rice and worshipping it with devotion is beneficial. Even the thumb can be the object of devotion. The Lord Shiva gives benefits based on the effort put in. One can also give a Linga or give money for its construction. Whatever one gifts a Shiva devotee with true faith, grants them access to Shiva's abode. One can also repeat 'Om' 10000 times or at dawn and dusk, also repeating 'Om' with 'M' helps purify the mind. During meditation the mantra has to be repeated mentally and in low voice for other times and this can also be done with the dot (Bindu) and mystical sound (Nada). Similarly the five syllable mantra can be repeated. The five-syllable mantra is especially powerful for Brahmins when started with 'Om'. A mantra must be obtained from a Guru.

The chapter also mentions some auspicious times for worshipping Shiva with the 'Om' mantra and it includes sun's transit to Kumbha. The mantras should be learned from a teacher. The Brahmins must start with 'Namah' in the mantras and others should end with it. If women repeat it 50 million times, they become equivalent to Sadashiva. Repeating it one or two or three or four crores of times, allows the devotees to reach the regions of Brahma etc. Doing it a thousand times a day for 1000 days gives one all desires. Feeding Brahmins and doing Gayatri mantra is also recommended. The study of Vedas and other mantras also allows one to reach Shiva. If mantra has only one syllable, it should be repeated one crore time before repeating 1000 times with full devotion. It is everyone's duty to repeat a mantra until death. Repeating "Om" a thousand times fulfils all wishes. Planting gardens for Shiva or keeping temples clean also leads to Shiva. One must reside in Shiva's temple and stay there till death as this grants one worldly and spiritual benefits.

The space around the temple has its own significance as temple built by ordinary people, holy space is 100 hastas; for sages its 1000 Aratnis; for gods its 1000 Aratnis and for self-risen Linga its 1000 Dhanuh Pramanas. Water bodies are considered Shiv Ganga and bathing, giving or mantra repetition there leads to Shiva. Obsequies, monthly offerings etc., if done in the holy centre, also lead to salvation. Staying there for a few nights also has its benefits. One gets results based on conduct, and caste, the higher the caste, the more benefits can be availed. Actions done with desire in mind yield immediate results. Actions done without desire result in Shiva's region. Rituals should be done in morning, rituals for desire in midday and those to suppress evil in the evenings. Worshipping in the middle of night yields good results. In Kali age only precise actions leads to results. People must be well behaved, and if that's combined with good deeds one reaches the right place. Suta concludes by saying that he will share the details of holy places and their traditions.

Chapter Twelve

(A TOUR OF SACRED SHIVA TEMPLES AND HOLY PLACES)

This chapter focuses on Suta describing the various sacred places, especially those with Shiva temples, where people can attain salvation. He begins by emphasizing that the Earth, which is vast, is filled with mountains and forests and it supports life through the blessings of Lord Shiva. He explains that Lord Shiva himself created these temples and sacred spots to help people achieve liberation. These places, whether naturally occurring or not, are special because they are frequented by saints and gods, making them powerful for spiritual growth and redemption. Suta emphasizes that performing acts of devotion like bathing, giving charity, and chanting mantras, in these holy places is very important. Failing to do so can lead to problems like diseases, poverty, and physical disabilities. He specifically mentions that if a person dies anywhere in India, they will be reborn as a human if they have lived in a holy place where a self-risen Linga (Shiva's phallic symbol) is present. He warns that committing sins in a holy place is very serious and one should strive to avoid any sin at all.

Suta then lists numerous sacred rivers, explaining their significance: The Sarasvati has 60 holy places on its banks, giving way to Brahma's region. The Ganga has 100 holy places, with places like Kashi (Varanasi), being particularly important, along with the holy periods of Margashirsha and when Jupiter is in Capricorn. The Sonabhadra has ten mouths and grants all desires, and the Narmada is a great river with twenty-four mouths, whose banks lead to Vishnu's region. The Tamasa and Reva have twelve and ten mouths, respectively. Godavari is a sacred river with 21 mouths, washing away sins like killing a Brahmin or a cow, and leads to Rudra's world. Krishnaveni has 18 mouths and leads to the world of Vishnu, and Tungabhadra has 10 mouths, leading to Brahma's realm. The

Suvarnamukhari has nine mouths. Suta also highlights rivers like Sarasvati, Pampa, Kanya, and Svetanadi, which lead to Indra's realm. The Kaveri River with its twenty-seven mouths is said to grant all desires and lead to the worlds of Brahma and Vishnu.

The devotees of Shiva are said to bestow Shiva's world. Suta describes several auspicious timings: When Jupiter and the sun are in the zodiac sign of Aries, bathing at Naimisha and Badara will lead to Brahma's world. When the Sun is in Cancer or Leo, bathing in the Indus will give knowledge. Bathing in the Godavari when Jupiter is also in Leo is special as Shiva himself has said that it bestows Shiva's world.

The Yamuna and Sona rivers are important when Jupiter and the sun are in Virgo and lead to the worlds of Dharma and Ganesha. The Kaveri river with Jupiter and sun in Libra grants all desires. When Jupiter is in Scorpio and sun is also there the Narmada river gives Vishnu's world. With Jupiter and Sun in Sagittarius, the Suvarnamukhari grants access to Shiva's world. And finally, Ganga when Jupiter is in Capricorn with Sun in Sagittarius gives knowledge after enjoying the worlds of Brahma and Vishnu.

Additionally, Suta says that performing obsequies with sesame seeds in Magha will give merit to both the parental and maternal side. Krushnaveni is also important when Sun and Jupiter are in Pisces. He adds that bathing in different sacred waters will grant the realm of Indra and that the Ganga and Kaveri rivers will absolve sins. Rivers like Tamraparni and Vegavati lead to Brahma's world.

Suta emphasizes that good behaviour, right thoughts, good intentions and compassion are crucial to receiving the full benefits of these holy places and that any sins done will be amplified. Sins done for livelihood may be negated by merit, but mental sins, are difficult to erase. Mental sins can be erased only by meditation, verbal sins through chanting, physical sins by weakening the body, and monetary sins by charitable gifts. He also points out the three stages of merit and demerit which include seed stage, flourishing stage and enjoyment stage. If they are in the seed stage they can be quelled by knowledge, in flourishing stage through penance and if it is in enjoyment stage it must be experienced and then destroyed. Worship, charity, and penance make the experience bearable. He concludes that people must refrain from sins to obtain peace and happiness.

Chapter Thirteen

(DOING WHAT'S RIGHT: EMPHASIZES MORALITY AND GOOD ACTIONS.)

This chapter of the Shiv Purana, focusing on good conduct, starts with a question from wise **sages**. They asked: *"**Please tell us how a sensible person can quickly reach higher realms and explain the good and bad actions that lead to heaven or hell.**"*

Then, **Sage Suta** answered their question. He began by explaining different types of Brahmins based on their knowledge and behavior. A true Brahmin knows the Vedas and acts virtuously. He described lesser Brahmins who might only know a little or not follow good conduct strictly, even comparing some to workers. Similar descriptions were given for other groups like rulers (Kshatriyas) and merchants (Vaishyas). Everyone, regardless of their role, should wake up early, meditate on gods, and think about doing good deeds. Even the first thing you see upon waking can hint at how your day will go!

Suta then detailed daily routines for good conduct. This included going to the toilet respectfully, cleaning oneself with water and mud in a specific way, washing hands and mouth, and cleaning teeth with a twig without using the index finger. Bathing is also important, sometimes involving special cloths and reciting mantras (prayers).

Prayer is a key aspect of good conduct, according to **Suta**. He emphasized performing "Sandhya" prayers at sunrise and sunset. Missing these prayers requires making amends by repeating the Gayatri mantra extra times. Repeating this mantra, especially in the morning, is crucial for Brahmins, and they should understand its meaning, connecting their soul to the divine.

Suta also talked about ethical behavior. He advised against hurtful speech and gossiping. He stressed helping those in need to the best of one's ability. Managing wealth responsibly is also part of good conduct. **Suta** explained that one should earn honestly and give a portion of their earnings to charity, with the amount depending on how the wealth was acquired. Giving food, water, and necessities is a great act of kindness. He also advised on dividing wealth for good deeds, growth, and responsible enjoyment.

Finally, **Sage Suta** concluded by stating that good conduct leads to happiness, while bad conduct leads to suffering. Following these guidelines for daily routines, prayers, ethical behavior, and managing wealth is essential for living a virtuous life and achieving a better future.

Chapter Fourteen

(UNDERSTANDING FIRE SACRIFICE AND OTHER WORSHIP.)

This chapter of the Shiv Purana explains different ways to offer sacrifices and worship, which are all ways to please the divine and get good things in return. The wise sages asked **Suta** to explain fire sacrifices, sacrifices to gods, studying Vedas, respecting teachers, and pleasing Brahmins.

Suta explained that offering things into a sacred fire is called fire sacrifice (Agniyajna). Young students collect special twigs and offer them in the fire. People who have given up worldly life offer their simple meals as a sacrifice. Householders keep a sacred fire burning in their homes and make offerings in it every evening and morning. Evening offerings are for the fire god and bring good fortune, while morning offerings are for the sun god and bring long life. Other offerings in the fire to please gods like Indra are called sacrifice to gods (Devayajna).

Suta also mentioned that simply studying the Vedas is a kind of sacrifice called Brahmayajna, and everyone should do it to please the gods. He then described how Lord Shiva created the days of the week for our benefit and assigned different gods to each day. Worshipping these gods on their specific day brings particular benefits: worshipping the Sun on Sunday brings good health, Lakshmi on Monday brings wealth, Kali on Tuesday removes sickness, Vishnu on Wednesday brings nourishment, Brahma on Thursday brings long life, other gods on Friday bring worldly pleasures, and Rudra on Saturday prevents untimely death.

Suta explained that there are five ways to worship these gods: repeating their special prayers (mantras), offering sacrifices, giving to charity, practicing self-discipline (austerities), and showing devotion through rituals at a sacred place, to an idol, in the fire, or by honoring a Brahmin. Doing the later forms of worship is more powerful than the earlier ones. If you can't do one, you can do another. For example, if you have eye or head problems, or even leprosy, you can worship the Sun and feed Brahmins for a certain period.

Suta concluded by saying that worshipping gods in these ways brings all sorts of good things. Brahmins should perform worship with special prayers, while others can use gestures. Rich people can worship by spending money, while those who are poor can worship through self-discipline. Doing good deeds leads to enjoyment in heaven and then rebirth in this world. Those with wealth should also plant trees and build water tanks for the benefit of others. Anyone who hears, reads, or helps others hear this chapter will get the benefits of offering sacrifices to the gods.

Chapter Fifteen

(DESCRIPTION OF THE QUALIFICATION, TIME AND PLACE FOR DEVAYAJNA.)

This chapter of the Shiv Purana tells us about the best places, times, and people for doing good deeds like fire sacrifices and giving to charity. The wise sages asked **Suta** to explain the best locations and times for these actions.

Suta explained that doing good deeds in a clean house is good, but doing them in a cowshed is ten times better. Giving near a pond, or at the base of a Tulsi, Bilva, or Asvattha tree is even more beneficial. Temples, riverbanks (especially holy rivers like the Ganga, Godavari, Kaveri, etc.), and seashores are increasingly better places. The very best place is wherever you feel most at peace. He also explained that good deeds were most effective in earlier times (like the Krita Yuga) and become less effective as time goes on into the Kali Yuga.

Suta also described good times for these acts. Holy days are good, but the time when the sun moves from one zodiac sign to another is ten times better. Even better are the times of the equinoxes (when day and night are equal), the start of the sun›s journey north or south, and lunar eclipses. Solar eclipses are especially powerful times for cleansing and giving because they can also bring negative effects. Spending time with wise and holy people is even more powerful than millions of solar eclipses!

Suta explained who is worthy of receiving charity. Someone who protects the giver from falling into bad karma is a worthy recipient. A Brahmin who has repeated the Gayatri mantra many times is pure and can help others. Giving food to anyone who is hungry is always good. It›s best to invite a good Brahmin with respect and give generously. Giving to someone who asks is good, but giving without being asked is even better.

Suta then described the rewards of giving to different kinds of people. Giving to a poor Brahmin brings worldly pleasures, while giving to a Brahmin who knows the Vedas brings heavenly pleasures. Giving to a Brahmin who chants the Gayatri mantra brings even higher rewards. He also talked about different kinds of «clean wealth,» with wealth earned honestly being the best.

Finally, **Suta** listed things that are good to give as charity throughout the year, like cows, land, seeds, gold, ghee, clothes, food, and even a virgin (in the context of marriage). Giving different things brings different benefits, like good health, strength, and long life. Even small acts like being kind to others› senses are a form of giving. Ultimately, doing anything with dedication to the divine brings good results. Reading or hearing this chapter makes you righteous and knowledgeable.

Chapter Sixteen

(DIFFERENT MODES OF WORSHIP OF CLAY IDOLS AND THEIR RESULTS.)

This chapter from the Shiv Purana explains how to worship God using clay idols and the benefits you can get from it. The wise sages asked **Suta** about the proper way to worship clay idols and what good things come from it.

Suta happily explained that this kind of worship brings all kinds of wealth and quickly gets rid of sadness. It can even prevent untimely death and bring you things like family, riches, and food. Both men and women can do this worship. The clay used to make the idol should be taken from riverbeds, lakes, or wells. It should be cleaned well and mixed with fragrant powder and milk. You should then carefully shape the idol with your hands on a raised platform, making sure all its parts and weapons look right. The idol should be sitting in a lotus pose, ready to be worshipped.

Usually, the five main gods – Ganesha, the Sun, Vishnu, Parvati, and Shiva – are worshipped in this way. However, Brahmins should always worship Shiva in his symbolic form, the **lingam**. To get the most out of the worship, you should offer sixteen different kinds of service to the idol, like sprinkling water with flowers and pouring water while chanting prayers.

The food offered should be good quality cooked rice. The amount of rice depends on where you are worshipping: a small amount at home, more in a temple built by people, even more in a temple considered holy, and the most in a self-manifested idol. Doing this worship many times can bring great rewards. Giving the idol a bath cleanses your soul, applying fragrant paste brings good qualities, offering food gives long life and satisfaction, and burning incense brings wealth. Lighting a lamp brings knowledge, and offering betel leaves brings enjoyment. So, these six things are essential in any worship. Bowing down to the deity and repeating special prayers (mantras) at the end of the worship fulfills all your desires, whether you want worldly pleasures or spiritual liberation. Worshipping different gods brings different benefits.

Worshipping Ganesha helps you achieve your wishes in this life. Worshipping Shiva, Vishnu, Parvati, and the Sun on their special days helps purify your soul. Certain days of the week, dates, and star positions are particularly good for worshipping specific deities. For example, worshipping Ganesha on Fridays or specific days in certain months is good. Worshipping the Sun on Sundays brings special benefits, and worshipping Vishnu on Wednesdays brings wealth and fulfills desires.

Similarly, worshipping Parvati on Mondays brings worldly pleasures, and worshipping Shiva on Sundays or specific days can fulfill all your wishes and bring long life.

The chapter also talks about a special offering called **Mahanaivedya**, which includes a large amount of rice, spices, honey, ghee, lentils, sweets, curd, milk, coconuts, betel nuts, cloves, camphor, and special flowers. Giving this offering and sharing it with others brings great rewards. Giving this offering many times can even lead to liberation from rebirth.

Finally, the chapter emphasizes the importance of worshipping the **Shiva lingam** to avoid being born again. The lingam symbolizes the union of Shiva and Shakti, the divine masculine and feminine energies. By worshipping the lingam with devotion, you can achieve great bliss and liberation. Reading or listening to this chapter helps you develop strong and lasting devotion.

Chapter Seventeen

(EXPLORING THE POWER OF OM AND THE FIVE SYLLABLE MANTRA)

This chapter of the Shiv Purana explains the power of the sacred sound "Om" and the five-syllable mantra "Namah Shivaya," both powerful tools to connect with the divine. The wise sages asked **Suta** to reveal the greatness of «Om,» the six Lingas, and the way to worship Shiva›s devotees.

Suta explained that «Om» is like a boat that helps you cross the difficult ocean of life and reach salvation. The sound «Om» is called Pranava and has two forms: a single, subtle sound, and a longer sound made of five syllables. The subtle form is for those who have already achieved spiritual freedom, and just reciting it can bring them closer to Shiva. The gross form, with its five distinct parts, is for everyone else. If you repeat "Om" many times with devotion, you can purify yourself, control the five elements (earth, water, fire, air, and space), and get a new understanding of your soul. Repeating "Om" for nine crores of times helps one to win over the elements.

The five-syllable mantra "Namah Shivaya," which means "I bow to Shiva," is another powerful way to connect with Lord Shiva. It is also considered as the gross form of Pranava. Chanting this mantra, especially as taught by a spiritual teacher, helps you gain many benefits. This practice is a great way to purify oneself.

Suta described the proper way to chant the mantra, emphasizing a clean place, proper posture, control of senses and a peaceful mind, also, the importance of the guidance of a Guru for the practice of this mantra was stressed. If you chant it a thousand times, you can free yourself from debts. If you chant it five hundred thousand times while visualizing the beautiful form of Lord Shiva, with the moon on his head, Ganga in his hair, and Shakti by his side, you can receive all kinds of blessings. The chapter also talks about a special ceremony where devotees of Shiva are honored. After this ceremony, they should offer a grand sacrifice. Then, you should honor these devotees and take a ritualistic bath in the water that washed their feet, which is more purifying than bathing in many holy rivers. Also, gifts of food should be given to these devotees with great respect. It was said that worshipping the wife of the Guru is like worshipping the goddess.

By doing the Japa (repetition) of this mantra many times, you can go to different worlds, beginning with earthly realms, then Vishnu's realms, and ultimately reaching Sivaloka, the highest abode of Shiva, where you merge with the divine. The chapter mentions that there are different levels of spiritual practitioners: those who follow rituals (Kriyayogin), those who practice self-discipline (Tapoyogin), and those who chant mantras (Japayogin). It emphasizes that it is only through devotion that one is able to achieve liberation.

Suta explained that the chapter›s teachings apply to everyone, even women and those of different castes can progress towards liberation. It is through the path of devotion to Siva through Japa, and by understanding the importance of the Linga that one is able to achieve salvation. He then concludes by stating that those who read this chapter or listen to its teachings will develop lasting devotion and ultimately merge with Lord Shiva.

Chapter Eighteen

(UNDERSTANDING FREEDOM AND ENTANGLEMENT: THE IMPORTANCE OF THE SHIVA LINGA)

The wise sages, eager for spiritual knowledge, respectfully asked the learned Suta a fundamental question: **What is the nature of being bound (bondage) and becoming free (liberation)?** They sought a clear explanation that would illuminate the path from worldly entanglement to spiritual freedom. They addressed Suta as someone who knows everything, highlighting their deep respect and the importance of the answer they were seeking.

Suta, in response to the sages' query, began by clearly defining bondage as being trapped by the "noose" of eight basic elements like our fundamental nature and ego. He explained that liberation is the state of being free from these elements. He elaborated that truly being free means completely controlling our inner selves and the forces of nature. Suta described how we are stuck in a continuous cycle of birth and action due to these binding elements. He emphasized that to break free from this cycle, we must worship Lord Shiva, who is the creator and master of this very cycle and exists beyond these binding elements.

Suta explained that worshipping Shiva – whether in the form of a Shiva Linga, an image, or even his devotees – with sincere devotion can please Him and earn His grace. This grace gradually helps us gain control over the binding elements, eventually leading to different levels of liberation, from simply residing in Shiva's world to ultimately becoming one with Him. He stressed the importance of performing sacred rituals, chanting Shiva's mantras, and constantly meditating on Him.

Suta then detailed various aspects of Shiva worship, including the significance of the Shiva Linga and its different forms. He spoke about the importance of sacred ash (Bhasma) and how applying it symbolizes realizing Shiva's essence within ourselves. He also highlighted the crucial role of the Guru (spiritual teacher) as a representative of Shiva who guides disciples towards liberation. Furthermore, Suta explained the need to worship Lord Ganesha and other deities to remove obstacles before undertaking sacred acts.

Finally, Suta elaborated on the **Santi Yajña (fire sacrifice)** as a means to purify oneself from negative influences and calamities. He described the process of setting up the sacred space, invoking deities, and offering specific items into the fire while chanting mantras. Besides the fire sacrifice, he also mentioned other powerful devotional practices like Kneeling down before Shiva and walking around, the Shiva Linga, as ways to destroy sins and draw closer to the divine. He concluded by emphasizing that a devoted life focused on Shiva, filled with virtuous actions and purity, is the path to true liberation.

Chapter Nineteen

(THE SPECIAL POWER OF SHIVA'S EARTHLY FORM I.E., PARTHIV LINGAM)

The wise sages, full of respect, praised Suta for explaining the greatness of Shiva's symbolic form, the Shiva Linga. Now, they asked him to share the special significance of the Shiva Linga made of earth, saying it must be even more powerful than the others.

Suta, happy to share his wisdom, told the sages that the **earthen Shiva Linga (Parthiv Lingam)** is truly the best of all forms. He explained that many great beings, including gods like Vishnu and Brahma, as well as wise people, achieved their goals by worshipping this simple, earthy form. Even different kinds of beings, like gods, demons, humans, and mythical creatures, attained greatness through its worship. He mentioned that in different ages, different materials were considered most special for the Linga, but in this current age, the **Kali Yuga**, the earth-made Linga is the most important.

Suta compared the earthen Linga to other incredibly sacred things. Just like Shiva is the most ancient and supreme God, the earthen Linga is the best form to worship him. Like the holy river Ganga is the greatest river, this Linga is the most excellent. Like the sacred sound "Om" is the most powerful mantra, this earthy form is the most worthy of worship. He continued, comparing it to the importance of Brahmins, the holy city of Kashi, the festival of Shivaratri, and Shiva's divine energy — all to emphasize its supreme position. He stressed that if someone ignores worshipping the earthen Linga and worships other gods instead, their worship is pointless. Doing good deeds like bathing in holy waters or giving charity won't truly help them.

Worshipping the earthen Linga brings purity, happiness, long life, satisfaction, nourishment, and good luck. Anyone with strong faith can worship it with whatever they can easily offer. If someone builds a nice platform to worship the earthen Linga, they will become wealthy and respected in this life and, in the end, become like Rudra (a form of Shiva). Someone who worships this Linga three times a day will enjoy great happiness for many future lives. They will be honored in Shiva's heavenly abode (Rudraloka) in their very body, and just by seeing or touching them, others' sins will be removed. Such a person is considered truly free even while living, wise, and like Shiva himself.

Suta further explained that whoever worships the earthen Linga daily, as long as they visited Shiva's temple in their life, they will stay in Shiva's world for that long. If they desire to be reborn, they will be a powerful king in India. But if someone worships the earthen Linga every day without wanting anything in return, they will stay in Shiva's world forever, achieving the highest form of liberation, becoming one with Shiva. Suta even warned that if a Brahmin doesn't worship the earthen Linga, they will suffer in a terrible hell.

Finally, Suta explained how the Linga should be made. It should be crafted carefully as one solid piece. If it's made by joining pieces, the worship won't be fruitful. This rule applies to Lingas made of gems, gold, or other materials as well when they are meant to be moved. However, Shiva Lingas that are fixed in one place are ideally made of two parts: the main oval part and the base. Those who mistakenly make a movable Linga in two pieces or a fixed Linga in one piece won't receive the benefits of worship. Therefore, it's important to create the movable Linga as a single piece and the fixed one as two, following the sacred rules. Worshipping a whole, movable Linga brings full rewards, while worshipping a two-piece one can be harmful. Conversely, worshipping a fixed Linga that is made of one piece not only fails to grant wishes but can also be dangerous.

Chapter Twenty

(THE MODE OF WORSHIP PARTHIV LINGA BY CHANTING VEDIC MANTRAS)

In this chapter Suta explains how to worship a Parthiv Linga, which is a Shiva Linga made of earth or clay, according to ancient Vedic traditions. Doing this kind of worship can bring both happiness in this world and spiritual liberation. To begin, a devotee should cleanse themselves with a bath and perform their daily prayers. Remembering Lord Shiva with deep devotion, they should then prepare to worship the Parthiv Linga following the Vedic rules to get the most benefit. This special worship should ideally take place in a clean and peaceful location, like the bank of a river, a temple, a mountaintop, or a quiet forest.

To create the Shiva Linga, the devotee needs to gather clay from a clean place. Traditionally, the color of the clay mattered based on social class, but if the specified color isn't available, any clean clay will do. The clay is then respectfully placed in a clean area, mixed with water, and carefully shaped into a beautiful Linga, following the instructions in the Vedas. This Linga is then worshipped with the hope of experiencing both joy in this life and ultimately achieving salvation.

During the worship, various items are made pure by sprinkling them with water while chanting the mantra "Namah Shivaya." Specific sacred verses (mantras) from the Vedas are chanted for different actions, such as making the water holy, making the worship area pure, and placing the Linga on its base. The devotee respectfully offers a seat for the Linga and invites Lord Shiva to be present there. Fragrant substances, rice grains, flowers (especially Bilva leaves), the smoke of incense, and a lit lamp are all offered while reciting special mantras.

Food offerings (called Naivedya) and fruits are presented, and everything is dedicated to Lord Shiva. Eleven grains of rice are offered to the eleven Rudras, again with specific mantras. A gift (Dakshina) is given, and the Linga is bathed with water while sacred verses are chanted. A lamp is waved in front of the Linga, followed by offering more flowers. The devotee then walks around the Linga in a clockwise direction as a sign of respect and bows down before it, touching the ground with eight parts of their body.

Different hand gestures (called Mudras) are performed while chanting specific mantras. These Mudras represent different aspects of Shiva. The devotee then silently repeats a powerful Shiva mantra or the entire Satarudriya mantra. Finally, after more prayers and chanting, the devotee performs a ritualistic farewell, requesting Lord Shiva to return to his divine abode.

This detailed method from the Vedas is one way to worship. There's also a shorter Vedic way that uses key mantras for each main step: bringing the clay, sprinkling water, making the Linga, inviting Shiva, and placing the Linga on its base. The other actions are done more briefly.

Finally, a simpler way to worship the earthen Linga is by chanting Shiva's eight names: Hara, Maheshvara, Shambhu, Sulapani, Pinakadhrk, Shiva, Pasupati, and Mahadeva. Each name is said with "Om" before it, used in a special grammatical form, and followed by "Namah." Devotees meditate on Shiva, picturing him in his divine form – like a silver mountain wearing the moon, holding an axe and a deer, and sitting peacefully on Mount Kailasa. They repeat the five-syllable mantra "Om Namah Shivaya" and offer sincere prayers, acknowledging that they depend on Shiva for their salvation. By worshipping Shiva with devotion in any of these ways, one can receive his blessings and achieve their desires.

(THE NUMBER OF SHIV LINGA TO WORSHIP FOR YOUR DESIRES)

In this chapter Suta Said: "You've already learned how to worship a Shiva Linga made of clay. Now, I'll explain how *many* of these clay Shiva Lingas you should worship to get specific things you desire in life. It›s said that if you worship other gods without also worshipping a clay Shiva Linga, your efforts might not bring the results you hope for. Your good deeds and charity might even be wasted. So, pay attention as I tell you the specific numbers of clay Shiva Lingas to worship for different wishes – these numbers are believed to definitely bring the desired outcome."

Remember, each time you begin worshipping a set of Lingas for a specific wish, the start of the worship, the placing of the Lingas, and the actual worship are all separate acts. Only the basic shape of the Linga remains the same. Everything else in the process is unique to that specific act of worship.

If you want to gain knowledge and become learned, happily make and worship one thousand clay Shiva Lingas. If you desire wealth, make and worship five hundred. To wish for a son, worship one thousand five hundred Lingas. For clothes and garments, worship five hundred.

For those seeking liberation or salvation, worship a crore (ten million) Lingas. If you desire land, worship one thousand. To ask for mercy, worship three thousand. If you wish to make a place a holy site, worship two thousand.

To gain friends, worship three thousand Lingas. If you want the power to control others, worship eight hundred. If you desire the death of an enemy, worship seven hundred. To enchant or attract someone, worship eight hundred.

To get rid of your enemies completely, worship one thousand Lingas. To make someone powerless, worship one thousand. If you want to create hatred between people, worship five hundred. To free yourself from troubles or difficulties, worship one thousand five hundred. If you are afraid of a powerful ruler, worship five hundred. If you are in danger from thieves or robbers, worship two hundred. If you're suffering from the bad influence of evil spirits, worship five hundred.

If you are suffering from poverty, worship five thousand Lingas. If you worship ten thousand Lingas, it is said that all your wishes will be fulfilled. Now, let me tell you about the daily practice. Worshipping just one Linga each day can remove your sins. Worshipping two brings wealth. Worshipping three is said to fulfill all your desires. Worshipping more than three each day brings even greater benefits, leading up to the promised results for the specific numbers I mentioned earlier. Now, I'll share another opinion from a different wise person.

An intelligent person can become fearless by making and worshipping ten thousand such Lingas. This can also remove fear of powerful rulers. A wise person can have ten thousand Lingas made to gain freedom from imprisonment. If you fear the influence of evil spirits, have seven thousand Lingas made and worshipped. Someone who doesn't have children can have fifty-five thousand Lingas made. To get daughters, have ten thousand made.

By making and worshipping ten thousand Lingas, a devotee can achieve the prosperity and glory of gods like Vishnu. By making one million Lingas, you can gain unmatched glory and wealth. It's said that if you make and worship a crore (ten million) Lingas, you can even become like Shiva himself.

Worshipping these clay Shiva Lingas is as powerful as performing a crore of sacrifices. It grants both worldly pleasures and spiritual liberation to those who desire them. Someone who wastes their time without worshipping these Lingas will suffer a great loss, no better than a wicked person. The merit of worshipping these Lingas is equal to all the charitable acts, sacred rituals, visiting holy places, self-control, and sacrifices combined.

In this current age, the Kali Yuga, worshipping the clay Shiva Linga is especially powerful and beneficial. There is nothing else quite like it. This is the conclusion of all our sacred texts and religious practices. The Linga grants both worldly happiness and freedom from the cycle of birth and death. It protects from all kinds of bad luck. By worshipping it, a person can become one with Shiva. Since even the wise sages are instructed to worship the Linga, everyone should worship it in the prescribed way.

These Shiva Lingas come in three sizes: excellent, medium, and small. The best Linga is about four inches tall with a beautiful base. The medium one is half that size, and the small one is half the size of the medium one. If you worship many of these Lingas daily with great devotion and faith, you can achieve any desire you hold in your heart. Among the four Vedas, nothing is considered as sacred as the worship of the Shiva Linga. This is the final understanding from all sacred teachings.

You can even abandon other rituals entirely. A truly knowledgeable person should focus on worshipping the Shiva Linga with great devotion. When you worship the Shiva Linga, it's like you're worshipping the entire universe, both living and non-living. There's no better way to save people drowning in the ocean of worldly existence. People in this world are blinded by ignorance and their minds are dirtied by worldly desires. Except for worshipping the Shiva Linga, there is no other boat to save them from destruction.

Gods like Vishnu and Brahma, sages, mythical beings like Yakshas and Gandharvas, perfected beings, demons, serpents, birds like Garuda, all the Manus, Prajapatis, and even humans have worshipped the Shiva Linga with great devotion to get the wealth and desires they longed for. People from all walks of life – Brahmins, warriors, merchants, laborers, and even those born from mixed marriages – should worship the Shiva Linga with the appropriate mantras.

Why should I say more? Even women are allowed to worship the Shiva Linga. Those who have been initiated into the higher castes can worship according to the Vedic rituals, but others who haven't been can also worship in simpler ways. Lord Shiva himself has instructed that those who are twice-born should perform worship according to the Vedic rules and not in any other way. However, some of these twice-born individuals, due to curses from sages like Dadhichi and Gautama, don't strictly follow the Vedic rules. But a person who rejects the Vedic ways and follows other traditions might not get the desired results.

A true devotee, after performing the worship as instructed, should also worship the eight cosmic forms of Shiva, which make up the three worlds: Earth, water, fire, wind, space, the sun, the moon, and the worshipper themselves. These eight forms are associated with different names of Shiva: Sarva, Bhava, Rudra, Ugra, Bhima, Isvara, Mahadeva, and Pasupati. Then, with devotion, the devotee should worship Shiva's attendants in the directions starting from the northeast, offering sandalwood paste, rice grains, and sacred leaves. These attendants are Isana, Nandi, Chanda, Mahakala, Bhrngin, Vrsa, Skanda, Kapardisa, Soma, and Sukra, with Virabhadra in front and Kirtimukha at the back. After this, the eleven Rudras should be worshipped.

Then, the devotee should repeat the five-syllable mantra "Om Namah Shivaya," the Satarudriya mantra, and many other hymns dedicated to Shiva. They should also recite passages from the Panchanga and walk around the Linga in a clockwise direction. After bowing down in respect, they should bid farewell to the clay image. This is how Shiva should be worshipped with true devotion.

For divine rituals, always face north during the night. Similarly, Shiva's worship should always be done facing north, not east. Sacred texts related to Shakti should not be recited facing north or west, as that is considered the back. Shiva should not be worshipped without applying the Tripundra (three horizontal lines of sacred ash on the forehead), wearing Rudraksha beads, and offering Bilva leaves. If ash is not available during worship, the Tripundra can be drawn with white clay instead.

Chapter Twenty Two

(WHO CAN EAT SHIVA'S NAIVEDYA AND WHY BILVA LEAVES ARE SPECIAL)

The Sages Asked: Wise Suta, we've heard before that food offered to Lord Shiva (Naivedya) shouldn't be eaten by everyone. Can you explain this more clearly? Also, tell us about the importance of Bilva leaves in Shiva's worship.

Suta Said: Listen carefully, all of you. I'll gladly explain these things. Those devoted to Shiva's sacred practices are truly blessed. A pure and dedicated follower of Shiva, who performs good deeds and is firm in their faith, *can* eat Shiva›s Naivedya. They should put aside any unworthy thoughts. Just seeing Shiva›s Naivedya can make your sins disappear. And when you eat it, you gain countless blessings instantly.

No number of ordinary sacrifices can compare to the benefit of eating Shiva's Naivedya. Eating it can help you become one with Shiva. If everyone in a family regularly eats Shiva's Naivedya, that home becomes holy and can purify others too. When Naivedya is offered, accept it happily and humbly. Eat it eagerly while thinking of Shiva. If someone hesitates to eat Shiva's Naivedya right away, thinking they can eat it later, they will commit a sin. Anyone who doesn't want to eat Shiva's Naivedya is a great sinner and will surely go to hell.

After being initiated into Shaivism (the worship of Shiva), a devotee should eat the food offered to the Shiva Linga, whether that Linga is imagined in the mind or made of materials like moonstone, silver, or gold. The Naivedya from any Shiva Linga is considered a great blessing and is auspicious for initiated devotees to eat.

Now, let's talk about who can eat Shiva's Naivedya if they are initiated into other religious paths but still devoted to Shiva. For certain Shiva Lingas, such as those made from Salagrama stone, those that are self-manifested (Rasalinga), or made of rock, silver, gold, crystal, or gems, as well as those installed by gods and enlightened beings, and special Kashmir Lingas and Jyotirlingas, eating the leftover food is like performing a purifying ritual called Chandrayana. Even someone who has killed a Brahmin can wash away their sins by eating the remains of food offered to these forms of Shiva.

However, for Lingas made of clay (Banalinga), metal Lingas, those considered self-born (Swayambhu), and other idols, permission from Chanda, one of Shiva's attendants, is usually required before the offering can be eaten. If Chanda's permission isn't there, devotees can eat the food with reverence. But never eat the offering where Chanda's permission is required.

If someone drinks the water used to bathe the Shiva Linga three times after the ritual, all three kinds of sins they've committed will be quickly destroyed. If there's anything from Shiva's offering that shouldn't be eaten, it's the part that was actually placed directly on the Linga. But anything that hasn't touched the Linga is pure and can be eaten. When the Linga is made of Salagrama stone, everything offered – food, leaves, flowers, fruits, or water – is pure and can be consumed.

Now that I've explained about the food offerings, listen attentively as I tell you about the greatness of Bilva leaves. This Bilva tree represents Shiva himself and is revered even by the gods. Its importance is hard to fully grasp. Every holy place in the world is said to be present at the base of a Bilva tree.

Someone who worships Mahadeva in the form of the Linga at the base of a Bilva tree becomes purified and will surely attain Shiva. If someone pours water over their head at the root of a Bilva tree, it's like they've bathed in all the sacred waters on Earth. They are truly holy. Shiva is very pleased when he sees the water basin around the Bilva tree's base full of water. A person who worships the root of a Bilva tree with fragrant substances and flowers will reach Shiva's abode. Their happiness will grow, and their family will prosper. Lighting lamps at the base of a Bilva tree with respect gives one the knowledge of truth and helps them merge with Shiva. Worshipping a Bilva tree with fresh, new sprouts frees one from sins.

If someone generously feeds a devotee of Shiva at the base of a Bilva tree, they receive ten million times more merit than usual. Giving a Shiva devotee rice cooked in milk and ghee at the root of a Bilva tree ensures that you will never be poor.

So, I've explained the ways to worship Shiva's Linga in detail. There are two main approaches: one for those still engaged in worldly life and another for those who have renounced it. Worshipping the base of the Linga fulfills the desires of those focused on the world. They should perform the complete worship in a vessel. At the end of the ritual, cooked rice should be offered as food. After worship, the Linga should be kept separately in a clean box in the house.

Those who have renounced worldly life should perform worship within the palm of their hand. They should offer the same food to the deity that they themselves eat. A subtle, symbolic Linga is recommended for those who have renounced the world. They should offer holy ash both for worship and as a food offering. After worship, they should always place the Linga on their head.

Chapter Twenty Three

(THE POWER OF SHIVA'S NAME, ASHES, AND RUDRAKSHA)

The Sages Asked: Wise Suta, devoted follower of Vyasa, please explain again the amazing benefits of holy ash (Vibhuti), Rudraksha beads, and the names of Shiva. By lovingly explaining these three, please bring joy to our minds.

Suta Said: It's wonderful that you've brought up this topic, which is so beneficial to everyone. You are blessed and holy, a credit to your families, because Shiva is your most beloved God. You always cherish the stories of Shiva. Those who worship Shiva are truly blessed and content. Their lives are meaningful, and their families are uplifted.

Sins can never touch those who constantly say the names of Shiva, like Sadashiva or Shiva. It's like fire can't touch burning-hot charcoal. When someone says, "Obeisance to you, holy Shiva," their mouth becomes as sacred as a holy pilgrimage site, destroying all sins. Just looking with love at the holy face of someone who says Shiva's name brings the benefit of visiting holy places.

Oh Brahmins, a place where Shiva's name is chanted, holy ash is present, and Rudraksha beads are found is incredibly auspicious. Just being near such a place gives the merit of bathing in the sacred Triveni (the confluence of three holy rivers). Shiva's name, holy ash, and Rudraksha beads are all very holy, like the Triveni itself. Seeing people who wear or possess these three is rare, but if you do, all your sins are washed away.

There's no difference between seeing such a holy person and bathing in the Triveni. Anyone who doesn't understand this is surely a sinner. A person who doesn't have holy ash on their forehead, doesn't wear

Rudraksha beads, and doesn't say Shiva's names should be avoided, just like you'd avoid a wicked person. As Brahma himself said, Shiva's name is like the Ganges River, holy ash is like the Yamuna River, and Rudraksha destroys all sins (like the Saraswati River).

Brahma, wanting to bless everyone, once compared these things. He put the benefit of having Shiva's name, ash, and Rudraksha on one side and the benefit of bathing in the Triveni on the other. He found them to be equal. That's why wise people should always wear these three. From that time on, Brahma, Vishnu, and other gods have worn these three, and just seeing them removes sins.

The Sages Asked: Oh righteous one, you've explained the benefits of Shiva's name, etc. Please explain it in more detail.

Suta Said: Oh Brahmin sages, you are all devoted to Shiva, with great knowledge and intellect. You are the wisest among the wise. Please listen with respect to the greatness of these three. This knowledge is hidden in sacred texts, Vedas, and Puranas. But because of my love for you, I'm revealing it now. Oh best of Brahmins, who truly knows the greatness of these three except for Shiva himself, who is beyond everything in the universe?

I'll briefly explain the power of Shiva's names, driven by my devotion. Oh Brahmins, listen lovingly to its greatness, the destroyer of all sins. Mountains of terrible sins are destroyed like a forest fire when the names of Shiva are repeated. They are reduced to ashes easily. This is true, undoubtedly true. Oh Shaunaka, different kinds of suffering caused by sins can only be stopped by chanting Shiva's names, and nothing else.

A person who is devoted to chanting Shiva's names is a true follower of the Vedas, a virtuous soul, and a blessed scholar. Oh sage, the sacred rituals performed by those who fully believe in the power of chanting Shiva's names bring instant results. Oh sage, people haven't committed as many sins as can be destroyed by Shiva's names. Oh sage, Shiva's names, when repeated, immediately destroy countless sins, even terrible ones like killing a Brahmin.

Those who cross the ocean of worldly life by using the boat of Shiva's names definitely destroy the sins that cause this cycle of birth and death.

Oh great sage, the sins that are the root of worldly existence are surely cut down by the axe of Shiva's names. Those who are suffering from the burning fire of sins should drink the nectar of Shiva's names. Without it, they can never find peace. Those who are drenched in the nectar-like rain of Shiva's names never feel bad, even in the midst of worldly troubles. Noble souls who have great devotion for Shiva's names instantly achieve liberation.

Oh lord of sages, the devotion for Shiva's names that destroys all sins can only be gained by someone who has done penance for many lifetimes. Salvation is easily reached only by those who have extraordinary and unwavering devotion for Shiva's names. I truly believe this. Even if someone has committed many sins, if they revere the chanting of Shiva's names, they will surely become free from all sins. Just as trees in a forest are burned to ashes by a forest fire, so too are sins destroyed by Shiva's names.

Oh Shaunaka, someone who regularly purifies their body with holy ash and chants Shiva's names can cross even the terrible ocean of worldly existence. A person who chants Shiva's names is not dirtied by sins, even if they have stolen from a Brahmin or killed many Brahmins. After studying all the Vedas, our ancestors decided that the best way to cross the ocean of worldly life is by chanting Shiva's names.

Oh excellent sages, why should I say so much? In a single verse, I'll mention the greatness and power of Shiva's names to destroy all sins: the power of Shiva's names to destroy sins is greater than the ability of humans to commit them. Oh sage, long ago, King Indradyumna, who was a great sinner, reached the excellent state of goodness through the influence of Shiva's names. Oh sage, similarly, a Brahmin woman who did many sinful things also reached an excellent state through the power of Shiva's names. Oh excellent Brahmins, I've told you about the supreme power of Shiva's names. Now, please listen to the greatness of holy ash, the most sacred of all.

Chapter Twenty Four

(THE AMAZING POWER OF HOLY ASH (VIBHUTI))

Suta Said: Holy ash, which brings good fortune, is of two main kinds. I>ll explain them to you now. Listen carefully. One type is called **Mahabhasma**, the great ash, and the other is **Svalpa**, the small or ordinary ash. Mahabhasma is further divided into three kinds: **Srauta** (from Vedic rituals), **Smarta** (from Smriti scripture rituals), and **Laukika** (made from ordinary fire). Svalpa is just the regular ash we see, which can come in different forms.

Only those who have been initiated into the higher castes (twice-born) should use Srauta and Smarta ashes. Everyone can use Laukika ash. Sages have said that the twice-born should apply holy ash while chanting mantras, while others can apply it without chanting. When dry cow dung is burned to ash, it's called Agneya, the fiery ash. This type is good for applying the Tripundra, the three horizontal lines on the forehead. Ashes from Agnihotra and other sacred fire rituals should be used for the Tripundra by those seeking wisdom.

When applying the holy ash to the forehead or smearing it with water, the seven mantras starting with "Agni" mentioned in the Jabalopanisad should be recited. People of all social groups and stages of life should apply the Tripundra on their forehead or dust their bodies with holy ash while reciting the mantras from the Jabala Upanishad. If they don't know the mantras, they should still apply the ash with reverence. Those seeking liberation should never stop dusting themselves with holy ash and applying the Tripundra in parallel horizontal lines. The scriptures say they should not be careless about this.

Shiva, Vishnu, Uma, Lakshmi, the goddess of speech, and other gods and goddesses, as well as people from all social groups, have always practiced applying the Tripundra and dusting with ash. Those who don't practice Tripundra and Uddhulana (dusting the body) properly cannot perform the duties of their social group and stage of life. Those who don't faithfully practice Tripundra and Uddhulana cannot be liberated from the cycle of birth and death, even after ten million lifetimes. Even after hundreds of millions of cosmic cycles, knowledge of Shiva will not dawn on those who don't faithfully practice Tripundra and Uddhulana.

It's the final conclusion of all sacred texts that those who don't faithfully practice Tripundra and Uddhulana are stained by great sins. Any action done by those who don't faithfully practice Tripundra and Uddhulana will have negative results. Oh sage, only great sinners who hate everyone develop hatred towards Tripundra and Uddhulana. After performing Shiva's sacred fire rituals, a self-realized devotee should smear their forehead with ash while reciting the mantra starting with "Tryayusha." The moment the ash touches their body, they become free from the sins of their bad actions.

Someone who applies the Tripundra with white ash during the three Sandhya periods (morning, noon, and evening) every day becomes free from all sins and rejoices with Shiva. Someone who makes the Tripundra on their forehead with white ash will reach the highest realms after death. No one should repeat the six-syllable Shiva mantra without applying ash to their body first. After applying the Tripundra with ash, they should begin the Japa (repetition of the mantra).

All holy places and sacrifices are always present wherever a person who has applied ash on their body stays, no matter if they are cruel, wicked, sinful, commit sins daily, are foolish, or have fallen from their path. Even a sinful person is worthy of honor by gods and demons if they have Tripundra on their forehead. How much more worthy is a faithful person with a pure soul! All the holy places and sacred rivers go to the place that a person with knowledge of Shiva who has casually applied ash visits.

Why should I say more? A wise person should always apply ash, always worship the Shiva Linga, and always repeat the six-syllable mantra of Shiva. Neither Brahma, Vishnu, Rudra, nor the sages or gods can fully explain the greatness of applying holy ash. Even if someone hasn't followed the duties of their social group or stage of life, even if they have missed sacred rituals, they will be freed from sin if they wear the Tripundra even once. Those who try to harm someone wearing Tripundra and perform their own rituals will not be liberated from worldly bonds, even after millions of births.

If a Brahmin wears the Tripundra with ash on their forehead, it's as if they have learned everything from their teacher and performed every sacred ritual. Those who feel like hitting someone upon seeing them with holy ash will be reborn to outcast parents. This can be understood by the wise. Brahmins and warriors should apply holy ash with great devotion to the parts of the body prescribed by the rules, while repeating the mantra "Ma nastoke." Merchants should apply the ash while repeating the Tryambaka mantra, and laborers with the five-syllable mantra. Widows and other women should do as the scriptures dictate.

Householders should repeat the Panchabrahma mantra, and unmarried students should repeat the Tryambaka mantra while applying ash. Forest dwellers should repeat the Aghora mantra, and ascetics should simply use the Pranava (Om). A Sivayogin, who is beyond social groups and stages of life because they believe "I am Shiva," should wear ash while reciting the Isana mantra. Shiva has ordained that the ritual of wearing ash should not be avoided by anyone, regardless of their social standing or even if they are outside the social structure.

A person who has applied ash to their body actually wears as many Shiva Lingas as there are particles of ash on them. Brahmins, warriors, merchants, laborers, people of mixed castes, women, widows, girls, those who follow different beliefs, unmarried students, householders, forest dwellers, ascetics, those performing sacred rituals, and women who wear the Tripundra are undoubtedly liberated souls. Just as fire burns whether you touch it knowingly or unknowingly, so too does ash purify whether you apply it consciously or unconsciously.

No one should eat or drink anything without applying Bhasma (holy ash) or wearing Rudraksha beads. If they do, whether they are a householder, forest dweller, ascetic, or belong to any of the four social groups or mixed castes, they become sinners and go to hell. If someone from the four main social groups repeats the Gayatri mantra, or if an ascetic repeats Om, they will be liberated. Those who criticize Tripundra actually criticize Shiva. Those who wear it with devotion actually wear Shiva.

Misery to the forehead without ash! Misery to the village without a Shiva temple! Misery to the life that doesn't worship Shiva! Misery to the knowledge that doesn't mention Shiva! Great is the sin of even seeing those who criticize Shiva, the support of the three worlds, and those who criticize someone wearing Tripundra. They are like pigs in a garbage heap, demons, donkeys, dogs, jackals, and worms. Such sinful people are hellish from birth. They may never see the sun during the day or the moon at night, even in their dreams. They can be purified by repeating the Vedic Rudra Sukta. Those who criticize a person wearing Tripundra are fools, and even talking to them can cause one to fall into hell, with no way to be saved.

Oh sage, someone who follows Tantric practices is not allowed in a Shiva ritual, nor is someone wearing the vertical mark (Urdhvapundra) of Vishnu. A person marked with a heated wheel (a Vaishnava symbol) is also excluded from Shiva rituals. As explained in the Brhajjabala Upanishad, there are many worlds to be attained, and knowing this, one should be devoted to holy ash. Just as sandalwood paste is applied over sandalwood paste, so too should only ash be applied over the sacred mark on the forehead. A wise person will not apply anything else over the forehead that wears the beautiful mark of ash.

Women should apply the Tripundra up to their hairline. Brahmins and widows should also apply the ash. Similarly, it should be applied by people in all stages of life. This bestows salvation and destroys all sins. Someone who properly applies the Tripundra with ash is freed from groups of both big and small sins. Unmarried students, householders, forest dwellers, ascetics, Brahmins, warriors, merchants, laborers, and even those considered low-born become pure through Tripundra and Uddhulana applied according to the rules, and their mountains of sins are destroyed.

A person who regularly applies ash is freed from the sins of killing women, cows, heroes, and horses. There is no doubt about this. Through Tripundra, sins like stealing, disrespecting others' wives, criticizing others, taking others' property, harming others, stealing plants, arson, accepting gifts from bad people, and having sex with forbidden partners are immediately destroyed. Stealing Shiva's property, criticizing Shiva or his devotees can be forgiven through rituals of expiation. Even an outcaste who wears Rudraksha and Tripundra is worthy of respect and is the most excellent of all.

Someone who wears the Tripundra on their forehead gains the same merit as someone who bathes in sacred rivers like the Ganga and all other holy ponds, lakes, and places in the world. The five-syllable mantra "Om Namah Shivaya," which grants union with Shiva, is equal to seven crore (seventy million) main mantras and many more smaller mantras. Oh sage, mantras of other gods that bring blessings are easily accessible to a devotee who wears the Tripundra.

Someone who wears Tripundra uplifts a thousand ancestors and a thousand descendants in their family. In this life, they will enjoy all worldly pleasures and live long without disease. At the end of their life, they will have a peaceful death. They will then take on a divine body with eight special qualities and travel in a divine chariot, attended by gods. They will enjoy the pleasures of celestial beings in the realms of Indra and other guardians, and finally reach Brahma's realm, where they will enjoy pleasures with celestial maidens. They will enjoy these pleasures for the entire lifespan of Brahma, and then enjoy pleasures in Vishnu's realm until a hundred Brahmas have passed. After that, they will reach Shiva's realm and experience eternal bliss, ultimately merging with Shiva. There's no doubt about this. After repeatedly studying the essence of all Upanishads, it's clear that Tripundra leads to great spiritual heights.

A Brahmin who criticizes holy ash is no longer a Brahmin but becomes low-born. They will suffer in terrible hells for the lifespan of Brahma. A person who wears Tripundra while performing rituals like Shraddha, Yajna, Japa, Homa, and the worship of gods is a purified soul and conquers even death. When bodily impurities are expelled, a water bath should be taken. A bath with ash is always purifying. A bath with mantras removes sin, and a bath with knowledge leads to the ultimate goal. A person who takes a bath with ash receives the same benefits as visiting all holy places.

A bath with ash is like a holy place where a bath in the Ganga is possible every day. Shiva is represented by the ash, which directly purifies the three worlds. Knowledge, meditation, charity, and mantra repetition are fruitless if a Brahmin performs them without wearing Tripundra. Forest dwellers, unmarried women, and those who haven't been initiated should apply ash mixed with water until midday, and dry ash after that. Someone who regularly wears Tripundra with a pure and controlled mind is a true devotee of Shiva and gains both worldly happiness and liberation. If a person doesn't wear Rudraksha beads, which bring many merits, and also doesn't wear Tripundra, their life is wasted.

I've briefly told you the greatness of Tripundra. This is a secret you should keep safe from everyone. Oh leading sages, the Tripundra consists of three lines on parts of the body like the forehead. The Tripundra on the forehead extends from the middle of the eyebrows to the tips of the brows on either side. A line drawn in the opposite direction with the middle and ring fingers is called Tripundra. Take ash with the three middle fingers and apply the Tripundra on the forehead. This will bring worldly pleasures and liberation.

Each of the three lines represents nine deities throughout the body. I'll tell you about them now. The nine deities of the first line are the sound "A," the Garhapatya fire, Earth, Dharma, the quality of Rajas, the Rigveda, the power of action, the morning rituals, and Mahadeva. Those initiated into Shiva's worship should understand this carefully. The nine deities of the second line are the sound "U," the Dakshina fire, the element of Ether, the quality of Sattva, the Yajurveda, the midday rituals, the power of will, the inner soul, and Maheshvara. Those initiated into Shiva's worship should understand this carefully. The nine deities of the third line are the sound "M," the Ahavaniya fire, the supreme soul, the quality of Tamas, heaven, the power of knowledge, the Samaveda, the evening rituals, and Shiva. Those initiated into Shiva's worship should understand this carefully. By bowing to the deities of the different parts with devotion, one should apply the Tripundra to become pure and attain worldly pleasures and liberation.

I've told you about the deities of the different parts of the body. Now, listen to the different places where the Tripundra can be applied. These lines can be made in thirty-two places, or half that (sixteen), or eight places, or five places. The thirty-two places are: head, forehead, two ears, two eyes, two nostrils, mouth, neck, two arms, two elbows, two wrists, chest, two sides, navel, two testicles, two thighs, two knees, two calves, two heels, and two feet.

The names of the following should be uttered when applying the Tripundra: Fire, Water, Earth, Wind, the directions, the guardians of the directions, and the eight Vasus (Dhara, Dhruva, Soma, Apa, Anila, Anala, Pratyusa, and Prabhasa). Or, the devotee can apply the Tripundra in sixteen parts of the body: head, forehead, neck, two shoulders, two arms, two elbows, two wrists, chest, navel, two sides, and back. The deities for these are the two Ashwins, Shiva, Shakti, Rudra, Isa, Narada, and the nine Shaktis. Or, the sixteen parts are: head, hair, two eyes, mouth, two arms, chest, navel, two thighs, knees, two feet, and back. The deities are Shiva, Chandra, Rudra, Brahma, Ganesha, Vishnu, Sri (Lakshmi) in the heart, Sambhu, Prajapati in the navel, Nagas, Nagakanyas, Rishikanyas in the feet, and the vast ocean in the back. Now, the eight parts: private parts, forehead, ears, shoulders, chest, and navel. The deities are Brahma and the seven sages. Or, the five parts for applying ash are: forehead, two arms, chest, and navel.

Considering the place and time, the devotee should do whatever is possible. If they can't dust their whole body, they should at least apply the Tripundra on their forehead while remembering the three-eyed Lord Shiva, the support of the three Gunas, and the creator of the three gods, by repeating "Namah Shivaya." They should apply Tripundra on their sides saying "Isabhyam Namah," on their forearms saying "Bijabhyam Namah," below saying "Namah Pitrbhyam," above saying "Namah Umesabhyam," and on their back and the back of their head saying "Namah Bhimaya."

Chapter Twenty Five

(THE AMAZING POWER OF RUDRAKSHA BEADS)

Suta Said *"Oh wise Sage Shaunaka, who embodies Shiva's qualities, please listen as I explain the power of Rudraksha beads. I will be brief. Rudraksha is a favorite of Lord Shiva, and it is incredibly purifying. Just by seeing it, touching it, or using it for chanting, all sins are removed.Long ago, Shiva, the supreme being, revealed the greatness of the Rudraksha to Goddess Parvati to help the world."*

Shiva Said *"Oh Shiva, Maheshani, listen to the greatness of the Rudraksha. I speak out of love, wanting to benefit my devotees. Oh Maheshani, I once meditated for thousands of divine years, with a focused mind. But, just for fun, and wanting to help the world, I opened my eyes. Tears fell from my beautiful, half-closed eyes. From those tear-drops, the Rudraksha plants grew. They became like trees, rooted in one place. To bless devotees, the Rudraksha plants were given to people of all social groups, who were devoted to Vishnu's worship. Rudrakshas that grow in the Gauda region are Shiva's favorites. They also grow in Mathura, Lanka, Ayodhya, Malaya, the Sahya mountains, Kashi, and other places. They can destroy mountains of sins, as declared in the scriptures. I instructed that these Rudrakshas should be divided into four types, corresponding to the social groups: Brahmins, warriors, merchants, and laborers. These Rudrakshas are naturally auspicious. The four types of Rudrakshas are white, red, yellow, and black, respectively. Everyone should wear the Rudraksha of their own group if they want to gain both worldly pleasures and salvation and if they wish to please Shiva.*

A Rudraksha that is the size of an Emblic myrobalan fruit is considered excellent; one the size of a jujube fruit is considered medium. Oh Parvati, listen lovingly for the benefit of my devotees: the smallest Rudraksha is the size of a gram. Even a Rudraksha that's as small as a jujube fruit brings blessings, happiness, and good fortune. One the size of an Emblic myrobalan destroys all troubles. One the size of a Gunja seed helps you get all your desires. Lighter Rudrakshas are more beneficial, and one that weighs only one-tenth is considered the most fruitful by scholars.

Wearing Rudraksha is good for destroying sins. It helps achieve everything you want, so you should always wear it. Oh Parameshwari, no other necklace or garland in the world is as auspicious and beneficial as the Rudraksha. Oh Goddess, Rudrakshas that are smooth, glossy, firm, thick, and have many thorn-like bumps bring worldly pleasures and liberation. Six types of Rudrakshas should be avoided: those with worm holes, those that are broken or cracked, those without bumps, those with cracks, and those that aren't perfectly round. The best Rudraksha has a natural hole from end to end. One that is made by drilling is medium in quality.

Wearing Rudraksha destroys great sins. If you wear eleven hundred Rudrakshas, you take on the form of Rudra himself. It's impossible to fully describe the benefits of wearing eleven hundred and fifty Rudrakshas, even in hundreds of years. A devoted person should make a crown of five hundred and fifty Rudrakshas. A pious person should make three circular strings, like a sacred thread, each with three hundred and sixty beads. Oh Maheshwari, three Rudrakshas should be worn on the topknot, and six in each ear. One hundred and one should be worn around the neck. Eleven should be worn on each arm, elbow, and wrist. Shiva's devotees should wear three Rudrakshas in their sacred thread, and five around the hips.

Oh Parameshwari, a person who wears so many Rudrakshas should be bowed to and worshipped like Shiva himself. Such a person, while meditating, should be seated properly and addressed as "Oh Shiva." By seeing this person, everyone is freed from sins. This is the rule for wearing eleven hundred Rudrakshas. If that many aren't available, I'll tell you another way. One Rudraksha should be worn on the topknot, thirty on the head, fifty around the neck, sixteen on each arm, twelve around each wrist, five hundred on the shoulders, and three strings each with one hundred and eight beads, like a sacred thread. Someone who wears a thousand

Rudrakshas and has a strong resolve in performing rituals should be bowed to by all gods, like Rudra himself.

One Rudraksha should be worn on the topknot, forty on the forehead, thirty-two around the neck, one hundred and eight over the chest, six in each ear, sixteen around each arm, and twelve or twenty-four around the wrists, depending on arm length. A person who wears this many with love is a great devotee of Shiva. They should be worshipped like Shiva and always honored by everyone. Rudraksha should be worn on the head while reciting the Isana mantra, on the ears with the Tripurusha mantra, around the neck with the Aghora mantra, and on the chest in the same way. The Rudraksha should be worn on the forearms with the Aghora Beej mantra, and a string of fifteen beads on the stomach with the Vamadeva mantra. With the five mantras starting with Sadyojata, three, five, or seven garlands should be worn. Or, all the beads can be worn with the main mantra.

A devotee of Shiva should avoid eating meat, garlic, onion, red garlic, potherbs, Slesmataka, garbage-fed pork, and liquor. Oh Uma, daughter of the mountain, Brahmins should wear white Rudraksha, warriors red, merchants yellow, and laborers black. This is what the Vedas teach. Whether someone is a householder, a forest dweller, an ascetic, or in any stage of life, they should follow this guidance. Only through great merit does one get the chance to wear the Rudraksha. If one misses this chance, they will go to hell.

Those who want good results should avoid wearing Rudrakshas that are the size of an Emblic myrobalan fruit, those that are lighter but have sunken thorn-like projections, those with worm holes, those without natural holes, and those with other defects. They should also avoid small Rudrakshas the size of a gram. Oh Uma, Rudraksha is a good addition to my Linga. The smaller one is always praiseworthy. People from all groups and stages of life, even women and laborers, can wear Rudraksha with Shiva's blessing. Ascetics should wear it with the Pranava (Om). If anyone wears it during the day, they are freed from the sins they committed at night. If they wear it at night, they are freed from daytime sins. The results are similar when worn in the morning, midday, or evening.

Those who wear Tripundra, matted hair, and Rudraksha will never go to Yama's abode."

Yama's Directive to his attendants *"Honor those who wear at least one Rudraksha on their heads, Tripundra on their foreheads, and repeat the five-syllabled mantra. They are truly holy. Bring here those who have no Rudraksha, no Tripundra, and don›t chant the five-syllable mantra. Always honor those who have ash and Rudraksha; never bring them here because of their power."*

Yama commanded his attendants like this, and they agreed in surprise. Therefore, oh Mahadevi, both the Rudraksha and the person who wears it are my favorites. Oh Parvati, even if that person has committed sins, they become pure. He who wears Rudraksha around their hands, arms, and head cannot be killed by any living being. They walk the world as a form of Rudra. They are always respected by gods and demons and honored like Shiva. By merely seeing this person, sins are removed from everyone. If someone is not liberated after meditation and gaining knowledge, they should wear Rudraksha. They will be freed from all sins and achieve the highest goal. A mantra repeated with Rudraksha is a crore (ten million) times more powerful. A person wearing Rudraksha gains a hundred million times more merit. Oh Goddess, as long as Rudraksha is worn by a living person, they will be safe from early death.

One attains Rudra by seeing someone with Tripundra, Rudraksha covering their body, and repeating the Mrityunjaya mantra. They are favored by the five deities and all gods. Oh beloved, a devotee should chant all mantras using Rudraksha beads or a garland made of them. Even devotees of Vishnu and other gods should wear Rudraksha without hesitation, especially those devoted to Rudra.

Rudrakshas come in various types. I'll explain their classifications now. Oh Parvati, listen with devotion. These Rudrakshas bring worldly pleasures and liberation. A single-faced Rudraksha is Shiva himself. It grants worldly pleasures and salvation. Just seeing it washes away the sin of killing a Brahmin. Fortune can't stay away when it's worshipped. Harms and distress disappear. All desires are fulfilled.

A two-faced Rudraksha is Isa, the lord of gods. It fulfills all desires and quickly washes away the sin of killing a cow. A three-faced Rudraksha always gives worldly enjoyment. Through its power, all wisdom is firmly established. A four-faced Rudraksha is Brahma himself. It washes away the sin of killing a man. Just seeing it or touching it brings the four aims of life. A five-faced Rudraksha is Rudra himself, known as Kalagni, the lordly one. It grants all types of salvation and fulfills every wish. A five-faced Rudraksha dispels all kinds of sins from sex with a forbidden person and from eating forbidden food.

A six-faced Rudraksha is Kartikeya. A man who wears it on his right arm is freed from the sin of killing a Brahmin. A seven-faced Rudraksha is called Anahga. Oh Goddess, by wearing it, even a poor person becomes a great lord. An eight-faced Rudraksha is Vasumurti and Bhairava. By wearing it, one lives a full life and becomes the trident-bearing lord (Shiva) after death.

A nine-faced Rudraksha is also Bhairava. Its sage is Kapila, and its presiding goddess is Durga in her nine forms, Maheswari herself. This Rudraksha should be worn on the left hand with great devotion. One will surely become like me. A ten-faced Rudraksha is Lord Janardana himself. By wearing it, all desires are fulfilled. An eleven-faced Rudraksha is Rudra himself. By wearing it, one becomes victorious everywhere. A twelve-faced Rudraksha should be worn in the hair of the head because all twelve Adityas are present there. A thirteen-faced Rudraksha is Visvedeva. By wearing it, all desires are realized. Good fortune and auspiciousness will come. A fourteen-faced Rudraksha is the supreme Shiva. It should be worn on the head with great devotion. It washes away all sins.

Oh daughter of the mountain king, I've explained the different types of Rudrakshas based on their number of faces. Now, listen to the mantras with devotion. (Mantras for each Rudraksha are given in the original text).

Om Hrīṃ Namah	Single-faced
Om Namah	2 faces
Klīṃ Namah	3 faces
Om Hrīṃ Namah	4 faces
Om Hrīṃ Namah	5 faces
Om Hrīṃ Huṃ Namah	6 faces
Om Huṃ Namah	7 faces
Om Huṃ Namah	8 faces
Om Hrīṃ Huṃ Namah	9 faces

Om Hrīṃ Namah	10 faces
Om Hrīṃ Huṃ Namah	11 faces
Om Krauṃ Kṣauṃ Rauṃ Namah	12 faces
Om Hrīṃ Namah	13 faces
Om Namah	14 faces

To achieve all desires, a devotee should wear the Rudraksha with mantras, devotion, and faith, avoiding laziness. If someone wears the Rudraksha without mantras, they fall into terrible hell for the duration of fourteen Indras. Upon seeing a person with a garland of Rudraksha, all evil spirits, ghosts, witches, malignant spirits, charms, and spells fly away, fearing a fight. Seeing a devotee with Rudraksha, Shiva, Vishnu, Devi, Ganesha, the sun, and all the gods are pleased. Therefore, knowing its greatness, Rudraksha should be worn while chanting mantras with devotion so that good qualities grow.

Thus, the power of holy ash and Rudraksha that bring worldly pleasures and liberation was explained by Shiva to Parvati. Those who apply ash and wear Rudraksha are Shiva's favorites. They are sure to enjoy worldly pleasures and salvation because of the power of ash and Rudraksha. Someone who applies ash and wears Rudraksha is called a devotee of Shiva. Someone who chants the five-syllabled mantra is a perfect and noble being. If Mahadeva is worshipped without Tripundra and Rudraksha, he doesn't give the desired results. Thus, I've explained everything you asked. The power of ash and Rudraksha brings fulfillment to all desires.

Someone who regularly listens to the auspicious stories of ash and Rudraksha with devotion will have all their desires fulfilled. They will be happy here, blessed with children and grandchildren, and will achieve salvation in the next world, becoming a great favorite of Shiva. Oh leading sages, I've now told you the essence of the Vidyesvara Samhita. As ordered by Shiva, it grants everything you want and also brings liberation.

RUDRA SAMHITA
SECTION I : CREATION

Chapter One

(THE INQUIRY OF THE SAGES)

This chapter begins with reverence for Lord Shiva, describing him as the source of everything, beyond the influence of Maya (illusion), and the embodiment of perfect knowledge. He is praised as the calm and tranquil being who created the universe and exists both within and outside of it, like space itself.

The narrative shifts as Vyasa mentions how Suta is about to describe Shiva after honoring the divine family of Shiva, Parvati, and their son Ganesha. Suta is then approached by sages in the Naimisha forest, led by Saunaka, who have heard the stories from the Vidyesvara Samhita. The sages express their thirst for more knowledge about Lord Shiva and humbly request Suta to share more stories of Shiva. They praise Suta's wisdom, gained through the grace of his guru, Vyasa.

The sages have several important questions. They ask about Shiva's true form – how a being beyond attributes (Aguna) can take a form (Saguna) in this world. They want to understand how Shiva maintains his form *before* creation, *during* creation, and *at* the time of dissolution. They are curious about how to please Shiva and what benefits Shiva bestows when he is pleased. They acknowledge Shiva's mercy and his inability to bear the suffering of his devotees. They also seek to understand the relationship between Shiva and the other deities, Brahma and Vishnu, noting that all three are born from Shiva, but Mahesa is distinct.

The sages also ask about Shiva's manifestation and activities, as well as the birth of Parvati and her marriage to Shiva. They want to know about their domestic life and their divine sports. They ask Suta to share everything he knows, leaving nothing out. Upon hearing this, Suta is delighted and, remembering Shiva's lotus-like feet, agrees to answer their questions.

Suta explains that the sages' inquiry is praiseworthy, as the stories of Shiva purify everyone – the narrator, the inquirer, and the listener, like the holy waters of the Ganga. He states that only those who are cruel, or 'slayers of animals', can be averse to hearing Shiva's stories. He compares this narrative to an antidote that heals the suffering of worldly existence, bringing joy and bestowing all desires. Finally, Suta states that he will explain Shiva's sports to the best of his ability, mentioning that Lord Vishnu, who is a form of Shiva, once asked Narada to question Brahma on the very same things. Hearing this, the sages become even more eager to hear this conversation.

The sages request Suta to tell them when and where this conversation between Brahma and Narada took place, what questions were asked, what answers were given, and how Shiva's glory was sung. Suta, pleased by their eagerness, agrees to narrate the entire conversation. This chapter serves as an introduction and sets the stage for further details on Lord Shiva, his nature, and his divine play in the following chapters.

Chapter Two

(INDRA SEND KAMADEVA TO DISTURB THE PENACE OF NARADA)

This chapter tells the story of how the sage Narada, son of Brahma, decided to perform a very intense penance (spiritual practice) in the Himalayas. He found a beautiful cave with a divine river flowing nearby, and set up a hermitage there. He meditated for a long time, focusing his mind, controlling his breath, and realizing his oneness with the ultimate reality (Brahman).

However, Indra, the king of the gods, became worried that Narada's intense penance might make him powerful enough to take over Indra's kingdom. So, Indra called on Kamadeva (Cupid), along with his wife Rati and his friend Spring, for help. Indra asked Kamadeva to go and disrupt Narada's penance by using his powers of attraction.

Kamadeva and his companions went to Narada's hermitage and tried to distract him with their powers, but Narada's mind didn't waver. This was because, long before, Lord Shiva had meditated in that very place and had burned Kamadeva to ashes for interfering with his penance. When Rati had begged for Kamadeva's life, Shiva had agreed to bring him back but also declared that the area would be free from Kamadeva's influence. So, Kamadeva was unable to have any effect on Narada's penance.

After this unsuccessful attempt, Kamadeva told Indra that Narada was too powerful. Indra was surprised and admired Narada but was still deluded by Shiva's Maya (illusionary power), unable to understand the true situation. It's explained that Shiva's Maya is incomprehensible and that everyone is deluded by it, except true devotees.

Narada, feeling proud of his achievement, believed he had conquered Kama. He went to Mount Kailasa to boast to Lord Shiva, thinking he was now equal to him as a conqueror of Kama. Shiva, being compassionate, advised Narada not to speak about his accomplishments, especially in front of Vishnu, because it was Shiva's own Maya that had protected Narada, not his own power. He also says that because Narada is a devotee of Vishnu, he is also his follower.

But, still under the influence of Shiva's Maya, Narada ignored Shiva's advice and went to Brahma's world. He told Brahma about his conquest of Kama. Brahma, understanding the true cause through his devotion to Shiva, also advised his son not to boast of his accomplishments, but Narada ignored this advice too. He then went to Vishnu's world, still filled with arrogance.

Vishnu, knowing Narada's purpose, welcomed him warmly and asked about his visit. Narada, feeling elated, boasted about his achievement once again. Vishnu, understanding that Narada is under the influence of Shiva's Maya, bowed his head, praised Shiva and then explained to Narada that lust and delusion arise only in the hearts of those who lack true devotion and that Narada was devoted to perpetual celibacy and had great knowledge and detachment and should be above those passions. By saying so, Vishnu wanted to remove Narada's arrogance. Narada humbly accepts what Vishnu had said and acknowledges Vishnu's power and then leaves.

This chapter highlights the power of Shiva's Maya, which can delude even great sages, and it emphasizes the importance of humility and true devotion. It also shows how Lord Shiva subtly influences events, all while testing and guiding his devotees.

Chapter Three

(NARADA'S HUMILIATION AT THE SWAYAMVARA)

The sages, after hearing about Narada's arrogance, ask Suta what happened after Narada left Vishnu. Suta, remembering Lord Shiva, begins to narrate what unfolded next. Suta tells them that Vishnu, knowing Shiva's intention, used his power of Maya to create a beautiful city with a wealthy king named Shilanidhi and his daughter, Srimati. This city was filled with wealth and prosperous people, and was much more beautiful than even the heavens.

King Shilanidhi was preparing for his daughter Srimati's *Swayamvara* (a ceremony where the bride chooses her husband). Princes from all over had gathered there, eager to win her hand. Narada, enchanted by the city, was also drawn by the sight of Srimati and her beauty and desire was kindled in his heart. He went to the palace, where the king honored him and asked him to examine Srimati's horoscope and foretell what kind of husband she would have.

Narada, now completely overwhelmed by desire, told the king that Srimati would marry a godlike figure, someone heroic, and equal to Shiva and Kamadeva. Having said this, Narada left the palace, consumed with thoughts of how he could marry Srimati. He knew that women are attracted to charming appearances, and he decided to go to Vishnu to get a beautiful form.

Narada went to Vishnu and asked for a form like his, so that Srimati would choose him. Vishnu, understanding the influence of Shiva's Maya, agreed but, as a subtle trick, granted him a form like Vishnu but with a monkey face, as Hari also means monkey. Vishnu then vanished, leaving Narada content but unaware of the deception.

Narada, believing he now had a beautiful form, went to the *Swayamvara*, where he sat among the other princes. He believed that Srimati would choose him because of his divine form. However, two of Shiva's attendants, disguised as Brahmins, saw the truth and, knowing Narada was deluded, mocked him. They pointed out to each other how Narada's body was like Vishnu's, but his face was like a hideous monkey.

Narada, blinded by his desire, didn't heed their mocking. Meanwhile, Srimati entered the *Swayamvara* hall with a golden garland in her hands, looking like Goddess Lakshmi. As she walked around, she was disgusted by the sight of Narada, with a beautiful body but a monkey›s face, and she averted her eyes. Failing to find a suitable match, she became distressed.

Just then, Vishnu appeared in the guise of a king, unseen by everyone except Srimati. Her face lit up, and she immediately placed the garland around Vishnu's neck. Vishnu, in the guise of a king, then took her and disappeared back to his abode.

The princes were left disappointed. Narada, still deluded, was agitated when the two disguised attendants told him that he had a monkey face and that Srimati had chosen someone else. Narada looked into a mirror and, seeing his ugly face, cursed the two attendants to be reborn as demons with Brahminical semen. The two attendants, understanding the influence of Shiva's Maya, remained silent, knowing that it was all Shiva's will, and quietly returned to their home and worshipped Shiva.

This chapter shows how Maya can delude even great sages, leading to pride and humiliation. It also highlights how Shiva's will is at play in every situation and that his devotees are protected, even when deluded.

Chapter Four

(NARADA CURSES VISHNU AND FINDS TRUE DEVOTION)

The sages, eager to learn what happened next, ask Suta about Narada after he was humiliated at the Swayamvara. They're curious about what Narada did after the two attendants of Rudra had left, and how he dealt with his rage. Suta, remembering Shiva, begins to narrate the next part of the story.

After cursing the two attendants, Narada looked into water and was surprised to see that his face was normal again. He was still deluded by Shiva's Maya, which made him think that Vishnu had tricked him. Completely enraged, Narada went to Vishnu's abode in Vaikuntha.

Narada angrily accused Vishnu of being wicked, deceptive, and envious of others' success. He reminded Vishnu of how he had once taken the form of an enchantress to trick the demons, and how Shiva had to drink poison to save the universe from the chaos of the churning of the ocean. He accused Vishnu of being naturally deceitful and claimed that Shiva was now regretting how much power he had given to Vishnu. Narada, full of arrogance and still under the influence of Maya, even threatened to teach Vishnu a lesson and then angrily cursed him.

Narada cursed Vishnu, saying that he would suffer separation from a woman in his human form and experience all the miseries of a human deluded by ignorance. Vishnu calmly accepted the curse, praising Shiva's Maya. Soon after, Shiva removed his Maya, and Narada suddenly regained his wisdom. He became aware of all his mistakes, and felt deep remorse for his arrogance. He cursed himself and praised Shiva's Maya, which had even deluded him.

Realizing his mistakes, Narada fell at Vishnu's feet and begged for forgiveness. He acknowledged his foolish actions and asked Vishnu to make his curse ineffective. He said that he was Vishnu's servant and that he was worried about falling into hell because of his actions.

Vishnu gently lifted Narada and assured him that he was a true devotee. He then explained that Narada's actions were a result of Shiva's will and that Narada should not feel too much guilt because it was Shiva who had made him act as he did. He told Narada that it was through his arrogance that he disobeyed Shiva's advice, and it was Shiva who caused him to act as he did. He said it was Shiva who removes pride, and that Shiva is the supreme reality, beyond all qualities, changes, and illusions. Vishnu explained that Shiva uses his Maya to manifest in three forms: Brahma, Vishnu, and Mahesa.

Vishnu further explained that the pure essence of Shiva is the cosmic witness who blesses his devotees. Vishnu told Narada how to gain true happiness, how to remove his sins, and how to achieve both worldly pleasures and liberation: he should let go of his doubts, always sing the praises of Shiva, repeat Shiva's hundred names, and always focus his mind on Shiva. Vishnu said that all sins vanish when someone chants Shiva's names. Vishnu said that Shiva is the only way to salvation.

Vishnu told Narada not to be sad as everything that happened, including the curse Narada placed on Vishnu, was Shiva's will. He explained that Lord Mahesvara was showing his divine conduct and is always working for the upliftment of his devotees. Vishnu said that there was no Lord more loving and inspiring than Shiva, who bestowed all power to him. He urged Narada to worship Shiva, listen to and share Shiva's stories, and worship Shiva's devotees.

He instructed Narada to always seek refuge in Shiva, as that brings ultimate bliss. Vishnu asked Narada to carry the lotus-like feet of Shiva in his heart, to go on pilgrimages to Shiva's holy places, and then to go to Kashi to worship him and finally to go to Brahmaloka to seek his father's wisdom. He asked him to specifically seek answers on the greatness of Shiva from Brahma. He assured Narada that Brahma would lovingly explain Shiva's greatness and reveal the hymn of a hundred names of Shiva. He asked Narada to become a devotee solely dedicated to Shiva as he would certainly be liberated by doing so.

After advising Narada, Vishnu, remembering, saluting, and praising Shiva, vanished from that place. This chapter highlights how Shiva's Maya can delude even the wisest, and the path of true devotion to Shiva as the ultimate path to liberation.

Chapter Five

(NARADA'S PILGRIMAGE TO KASHI AND QUEST FOR SHIVA'S TRUTH)

This chapter begins with Narada, now free from his delusion, wandering the earth and visiting various holy places associated with Shiva. He was filled with devotion and joy as he saw the many forms of Shiva that grant worldly happiness and salvation to devotees.

While Narada was traveling, the two attendants of Shiva, who Narada had cursed in the previous chapter, found him. By now, Narada's mind was pure. They bowed to Narada, touched his feet, and, wanting to be free from the curse, respectfully asked him for forgiveness. They explained that they were not ordinary Brahmins but attendants of Shiva. They reminded Narada that they had offended him when his mind was deluded and that they had remained silent, understanding that it was all a result of Shiva's will. They confessed that they were reaping the fruit of their actions and asked Narada to bless them.

Narada, now without anger, listened to them with love and replied that he knew his anger was due to Shiva's will and that he had cursed them under that influence. However, Narada then explained that his curse would lead them to great power: they would be born as demons from the semen of a powerful sage. They would rule the universe as devoted followers of Shiva, with their senses conquered, and they would regain their original position after being killed by a manifestation of Shiva.

The two attendants of Shiva, delighted by Narada's words, returned to their abode. Narada, now fully devoted to Shiva, continued his travels, visiting the holy sites of Shiva. He eventually reached Kashi (Varanasi), a city favored by Shiva that grants liberation. He was filled with joy and devotion as he worshipped Lord Shiva in Kashi. While staying there, he became peaceful, praising Shiva, remembering him with love and devotion, and finally deciding to seek further knowledge from Brahma.

Narada then went to Brahma's world. He bowed to Brahma and praised him, then asked him about the true nature of Shiva. Narada admitted that even though he had heard much about devotion, knowledge, penance, charity, and holy places, he still did not understand Shiva. He asked Brahma to explain the rules of Shiva's worship and to describe Shiva's various activities. He was also confused about how Shiva, who is beyond all attributes, could take on qualities in the world.

Narada questioned how Shiva existed in his pure form *before* creation, how he played during creation, and how he exists at the time of dissolution. He asked how one can please Shiva and what benefits he bestows upon his devotees when pleased. Narada noted that Shiva is considered very merciful and cannot bear the distress of his devotees. He also pointed out that Brahma, Vishnu, and Mahesa (Shiva) are all born from Shiva, and Mahesa, having all the qualities of Shiva, is actually Shiva himself.

Finally, Narada requested Brahma to explain Shiva's manifestation, his exploits, the birth of Uma (Parvati), her marriage, their domestic life, their divine sports, and the birth of Guha (Kartikeya). He admitted that he had heard these things before, but he was not satisfied and thus sought refuge in Brahma to fully understand these things. Brahma, pleased with his son's questions, prepared to answer. This chapter sets the stage for Brahma to explain Shiva's nature and his various activities.

Chapter Six

(THE GREAT DISSOLUTION AND THE ORIGIN OF VISHNU)

Brahma, pleased with Narada's sincere questions, begins to explain the nature of Shiva. He says that he, Vishnu, and no one else truly understands Shiva or his supreme forms. Brahma starts by describing the state of the universe at the time of *Mahapralaya* (the Great Dissolution).

At that time, everything dissolves into complete darkness. There is no sun, moon, stars, planets, day, night, fire, wind, earth, or water. Even the unmanifest, primordial being is gone. The entire space is a void, with no light or energy. There is no Dharma or Adharma, no sound, touch, smell, color, or taste. There are no directions. In this impenetrable darkness, only what the Vedas call "The Existent" or "Brahman" is present. This form is not understandable by the mind or expressible through words. It has no name, color, thickness, length, weight, or any other attribute.

This "Existent" is said to be everywhere, the ultimate truth, knowledge, and bliss. It is immeasurable, without support, unchanging, formless, and the cause of the universe. It is without beginning or end and has no other. After some time, this Being wished to create a second. In its own playful way, it decided to create an auspicious form full of power, qualities, and knowledge. This form should be all-seeing, all-powerful, the cause of everything, respected by all, and capable of bestowing and purifying everything.

So, this original formless Being created a new form: **SadaShiva**. This form, which is called **Ishvara**, is the manifest form of the formless Being, and ancient and future scholars have called it Ishvara. Ishvara, although one, created a physical form of Shakti from his own body, without affecting his body in any way. This Shakti is called by various names, such as Pradhana, Prakriti, Maya, Gunavati, Para, and Ambika. She is the mother of the cosmic intelligence and the goddess of all. She is the main cause and the mother of the three deities.

This Shakti has eight arms, a face as bright as a thousand moons, and thousands of stars that seem to always circle around her face. She wears many ornaments and holds various weapons. Her eyes are like full-blown lotuses, and she has a brilliance that cannot be imagined. The supreme Purusha is Shiva. He is called Shambhu and has no lord above him. He has the Ganges on his head, the crescent moon on his forehead, three eyes, five faces, and ten arms. He holds a trident and is as pure and white as camphor. His body is covered in holy ash.

This Brahman, in the form of Time, along with Shakti, created a holy place called Shivaloka, also known as Kalika, a seat of salvation that shines above everything else. This holy place is a place of pure bliss where the divine lovers always stay. Even during the Great Dissolution, this place is never without Shiva and Shakti, so it is called Avimukta.

Then, desiring to create another being, Shiva created another being. Shiva decided to create someone who could create, protect, and dissolve everything. This person would have all the responsibilities of the universe. Shiva spread nectar from the tenth part of his left side - a nectar that was the result of churning his mind, which was the ocean of thoughts, with the *sattva* quality being the gem, *rajas* being coral, and *tamas* being a crocodile. From this, a person appeared who was very charming, calm, and full of immeasurable majesty and was full of *sattva* quality.

This new being was patient, without comparison, with a sapphire-like complexion, brilliant eyes, a golden form, and wore two beautiful silk garments. He bowed to Shiva and asked for his name and task. Shiva laughed and told him that he would be known as Vishnu, as he is all-pervading. He told him to perform intense penance, and with that, bestowed the Vedas on him through his nostrils. Shiva then vanished with Shakti.

Vishnu, after bowing to Shiva, started his intense penance. Even after twelve thousand divine years, he could not get a vision of Shiva. Feeling suspicious, he meditated on Shiva and wondered what he should do. At that moment, Shiva told him to do more penance. Vishnu then performed a terrible penance, following the path of meditation and finally understood. He was surprised by the realization of "What is the True Entity". From Vishnu's body, who was putting so much effort, water began to flow as a result of Shiva's Maya. This divine water pervaded everything, and just touching it can destroy sins. The weary Vishnu went to sleep in this water. This is how his name became Narayana: "He who has water as his abode".

At the same time, the principles of the universe were born from the great soul. From Prakriti came Mahat (cosmic intellect), and from Mahat came the three qualities, and from there came Ahamkara (cosmic ego) in three forms, and then came the essences, the five elements, and the senses. Brahma says that all these principles that come from Prakriti are insentient, but the Purusha (Vishnu) is not. Vishnu accepted these 24 principles, according to Shiva's will, and went to sleep in the Brahman.

This chapter describes how Shiva is beyond everything, even the creation, and how the other deities, like Vishnu, are manifestations of his power and how he acts according to his will and makes others act so.

Chapter Seven

(THE DISPUTE BETWEEN BRAHMA AND VISNU)

This chapter begins with Brahma describing what happened after Vishnu fell asleep on the waters. A huge lotus flower grew out of Vishnu's navel, as desired by Shiva. This lotus was incredibly large, brilliant, and beautiful.

From his right side, Shiva, along with Parvati, created Brahma out of the lotus. But Shiva deluded Brahma with his Maya, making him think he was born from the lotus itself and not aware of his true source. Brahma was confused, wondering about his origins and duty. He decided to find out the source of the lotus by going down its stalk. He traveled downwards for a hundred years but couldn't find the source. Discouraged, he decided to climb upwards.

For another hundred years, Brahma traveled upward but still couldn't reach the top. He became exhausted and confused. It was then that he heard a voice from the sky, telling him to perform penance in order to see his creator. After twelve years of penance, Vishnu suddenly appeared before him, looking beautiful, with four arms, holding a conch, a discus, a mace, and a lotus.

Brahma, still deluded by Shiva's Maya, did not recognize Vishnu as his creator. He was amazed by Vishnu's beauty. He also could not recognize that it was Shiva's Maya who had made him be ignorant about his creator. He asked Vishnu who he was, and poked Vishnu to wake him from his slumber, with ever increasing force. Vishnu woke up from his sleep, with his lotus like eyes wet due to sleep and smiling sweetly at Brahma, called him "Dear Child".

Hearing Vishnu call him "Dear Child", Brahma became furious and, full of ego, declared that he was the creator of all worlds, the one who activates Prakriti, and the eternal, all-pervading Brahman, born from Vishnu. He claimed he was the soul of the universe and demanded an explanation for Vishnu's actions. Vishnu replied calmly that he knew Brahma as the creator, but that Brahma had come from his body for the purpose of creation and support of the universe, and that Brahma had forgotten that Vishnu was the true source of everything, and the ruler of the universe, the supreme soul. He said he was the origin, the preserver and the destroyer, and he has all the qualities of the universe. Vishnu said that he was the greatest light, the great Atma, and the omnipresent one and that he had created the **twenty four** Tattvas and that everything mobile and immobile was created by him and he asked Brahma to take refuge in him.

Brahma, proud of being Brahma, became furious upon hearing these words. He challenged Vishnu's claims and declared there must be a creator of Vishnu too. Because of Shiva's Maya, a great fight began between Brahma and Vishnu. Their fight continued for a long time in the vast sea of dissolution.

To stop their quarrel, a huge, fiery Linga appeared in front of them. This Linga had no beginning, middle, or end and was unlike anything they had ever seen. It had a thousand flames. Vishnu became unconscious due to the heat of the flames. When Brahma too became senseless, Vishnu suggested that they should stop fighting and examine the fiery column.

Vishnu said he would go down to find the root of the Linga, and Brahma should go up to see its top. Vishnu took the form of a boar and went down and Brahma took the form of a swan and went up. Vishnu, as the boar, traveled downwards for a thousand years, but found no end. From then on, he was known as **Svetavaraha**, the white boar. Similarly, Brahma flew upwards for a thousand years, but found no end. Both were exhausted and returned to where they had started. They were both deluded by Shiva's Maya.

They realized they could not understand the Linga and started praising it. They bowed at its front, sides, and back, acknowledging that they did not know its true form, and asked the Linga to reveal itself. They realized that this form could not be explained and it was without any action and name and that it was beyond all forms of meditation. Both Brahma and Vishnu, wanting to quell their earlier pride, performed the obeisance and prayer for a hundred Autumns. This chapter illustrates how the pride and ego of even the most powerful deities like Brahma and Vishnu were quelled by Shiva and his Maya.

Chapter Eight

(THE SOUND OF OM AND THE LETTERED FORM OF SHIVA)

Brahma continues to tell Narada about the time after his fight with Vishnu. He explains that both he and Vishnu were humbled and eager to see the true form of the Lord. They waited patiently, and Shiva, the protector of the distressed, showed mercy. A clear sound of "Om" arose from the fiery Linga, echoing loudly and clearly.

Brahma and Vishnu wondered about the source of this sound. Then Vishnu, with a joyful heart, saw a manifestation of the eternal being on the right side of the Linga. He saw the syllable "A" first, then the syllable "U," then the syllable "M," and finally, the complete sound "Om." He saw "A" like a blazing sun, "U" like dazzling fire, and "M" like a glittering moon. Above these, he saw the supreme Brahman, a pure crystal-like being beyond all limitations, without any beginning, middle or end, the source of Bliss and Truth. Vishnu realized that this supreme reality is both within and outside, and can't be fully expressed with words.

Vishnu meditated on this universal soul, surrounded by these Vedic sounds. He wanted to find the source of the fiery column. At that moment, a sage appeared and revealed the truth - that he himself was the supreme Lord, the Brahman embodied in the sound of "Om".

Brahma explains that Brahman is Rudra, free from worries, and beyond the reach of mind and words, but can be expressed through the single syllable "Om." The single syllable "A" is the source of Brahma, "U" is the source of Vishnu, and "M" is the source of Rudra. "A" represents the creator, "U" represents the enchanter, and "M" represents the one who always blesses. "A" is the seed of the universe, "U" is Vishnu, the source of all of existence, and together they are Shiva.

From the Linga, the source, came the seed "A". When this seed was placed in the source "U," it grew into a golden egg. This egg floated on water for many years, until it split in two and gave birth to Brahma. The top part of the egg became the heavens, and the lower part became the earth. Brahma, born from the egg, was expressed by the syllable "KA". He is the creator of all worlds. Those who know the Yajurveda call this "Om." On hearing the sound of the Yajurveda, those who knew the Rigveda and Samaveda called them Vishnu and Brahma.

Realizing the greatness of the Lord, Brahma and Vishnu then praised Shiva as best as they could. Vishnu saw another incredibly beautiful form: five faces, ten arms, white as camphor, and decorated with many ornaments. This was a form of Shiva himself with Uma.

Then, Lord Shiva showed them his form, which was made of letters. The letter "A" was his head, the long "AA" his forehead, "I" his right eye, "EE" his left eye, and so on, with different letters representing different parts of his face and body. This showed them the true nature of Shiva as the sound and the source of the universe.

Brahma explained that different mantras are associated with different sounds and actions. The mantra beginning with Om, with five parts and thirty-eight syllables, brings intelligence and success in sacred tasks. The Gayatri mantra with twenty-four syllables and four parts brings joy. A mantra with eight parts and thirty syllables is used for black magic. Yajurveda mantras with twenty-five syllables and eight parts are used for reconciliation. A mantra with thirteen parts and sixty-one syllables brings growth and destruction. Vishnu received five mantras from Shiva: Mrityunjaya, five-syllable, Cintamani, Dakshinamurti and "Tattvamasi" (the mahavakya of Hara). Vishnu then began chanting these mantras.

Pleased, Vishnu and Brahma praised Shiva, who they had seen in the form of sounds, syllables, and mantras. They described him as merciful, beautiful, hidden from all, auspicious, having a beautiful feet, covered with huge snakes, and extending all around, the Lord of Brahma, and the cause of the creation, sustenance, and destruction of the world. This chapter describes how Shiva manifested as the sound "Om" and the embodiment of all letters, showing that he is the source of all creation and knowledge.

Chapter Nine

(THE NATURE OF SHIVA AND HIS INSTRUCTIONS TO BRAHMA AND VISHNU)

Brahma continues his story, explaining that when Vishnu praised Shiva, the compassionate Shiva, full of kindness, revealed himself to them along with his consort, Uma. Shiva had five faces, three eyes, a crescent moon on his forehead, matted hair, and a white complexion. His body was dusted with ash, and he had ten arms. His neck was blue, and he wore many ornaments. He was beautiful in every way, with three ash lines marking his forehead.

Seeing Shiva and his beautiful consort, Brahma and Vishnu praised him again. Shiva, pleased by their devotion, breathed the Vedas into Vishnu and gave him the knowledge of the supreme Atman. Then, out of compassion, Shiva gave the same knowledge to Brahma. After receiving the Vedas, Vishnu humbly asked Shiva how to worship him, how to meditate on him, and how to impress him. He also asked what they should do according to his wishes.

Shiva, delighted by their questions, told them to see him as the great deity and cast aside all fear. He said they should worship his Linga (phallic symbol) and meditate on the form they were seeing at that moment, and that worshipping him in the phallic form would give people all that they desire. He said that any trouble that may befall them could be destroyed by worshipping his Linga. He told them that he was the Lord of everything, that Brahma was born from his right side, and Vishnu from his left. Shiva then promised to fulfill all their wishes, and that they should worship him by making his form out of clay, and by serving him they will attain happiness.

He asked Brahma to follow his direction and create the universe, and he asked Vishnu to sustain all living beings. Brahma and Vishnu, having understood the method of worshipping him, requested Shiva that their devotion for him should always be steady and unwavering. They requested him that he should manifest in various forms and help them and that even their dispute had now become auspicious as they had now witnessed him.

Shiva explained that although he is without attributes (Nirguna), he also has attributes (Saguna) and that he is the source of creation, maintenance, and dissolution. He said that he was the supreme Brahman, without decay or change, and that existence, knowledge, and bliss were his true nature. Shiva also explained that, for the sake of creation, preservation and destruction, he manifests himself into the three forms of Brahma, Vishnu and Rudra. He told Vishnu that because they had both praised him, he would fulfill their wishes for him to incarnate. Shiva also said that a form like him would come from Brahma, and that form would be called Rudra.

He said that Rudra would be his own part and that there would be no difference between him and Rudra and in their modes of worship. He used the example of fire and water to explain how his Nirguna aspect remains unaffected, no matter which form he manifests in and he explained that Shiva and Rudra are the same, as gold is gold no matter what ornament it may be shaped as and clay is clay no matter how many objects are made out of it. He explained that this truth is known by those of clear knowledge, and that those who realize this will not see any difference between the forms and he urged them to see Shiva as the fundamental material.

Shiva also revealed a secret: that he is Tamasa (full of ignorance) and Prakrta (a form of Maya), which becomes Hara with the Gunas. and Vaikarika (Ego). He further explained that the goddess Uma was his Prakriti, and that his speech would go to Brahma, his form of Lakshmi would go to Vishnu, and his power, Kali, would always be his Shakti. He explained that he was giving each of them a role with a Shakti and that all three of them would carry out his directions. He said that Vishnu would work with Lakshmi to maintain the universe, Brahma would create with his power, and Rudra, with Kali, would destroy it and that all of them should always work for the good of the world.

Shiva said that he would also bestow liberation at Vishnu's bidding and that the benefits of seeing Vishnu would be the same as seeing Shiva. He said he dwells in Vishnu's heart and Vishnu in his heart. He said that those who discriminate against him and Vishnu do not know his mind. He clarified that he manifests in three forms- Brahma, Vishnu and Bhava and that he creates, protects and destroys with the Gunas of Rajas, Sattva and Tamas, but he himself is beyond these Gunas. He explained how Sattva, Tamas and Rajas are used differently by the three deities.

Shiva told Vishnu to protect Brahma, that Rudra, the destroyer of the three worlds, was also an incarnation of Shiva, and that in the future Padma Kalpa, Brahma would be born as Vishnu's son. He then gave another boon to Vishnu and said that they all would meet at that time. This chapter explains that although Shiva is beyond attributes, he also manifests with attributes and that he is the source of all deities. He is the ultimate reality, and devotion to him leads to ultimate liberation.

Chapter Ten

(SHIVA'S FINAL INSTRUCTIONS AND THE POWER OF THE LINGA)

Shiva, pleased with Vishnu's devotion, begins this chapter by giving further instructions. He assures Vishnu that he will be honored and worshipped throughout the worlds forever and he will always be there to help him remove the miseries of the world and kill his enemies. He says that he would take the form of Rudra to perform the tasks that Vishnu can not and that Vishnu and Rudra are one and the same, and that any devotee of Rudra should also honor Vishnu. Shiva warns that anyone who hates Vishnu will go to hell. Shiva instructs Vishnu to be a bestower of worldly pleasures and salvation and to engage in acts that will bless and protect the world.

Shiva took Brahma and Vishnu by the hand and asked them to help all those in distress. He instructed them to be the presiding deities of everything and to grant worldly pleasures and liberation. He said they would take the form of vital air in everyone, and in times of distress, people should worship his form as Rudra, and that those who seek refuge in Vishnu also seek refuge in Shiva.

Shiva then explained the lifespans of the deities: a thousand sets of the four Yugas make up a day of Brahma, and his night is the same length. Brahma's lifespan is one hundred of these years. One year of Brahma is one day of Vishnu, and Vishnu lives for one hundred such years. One year of Vishnu is one day of Rudra. When a hundred years of Rudra pass, Rudra becomes Nara (the supreme man). He stays like that as long as Sadasiva holds his breath, and when Sadasiva exhales, Rudra merges into Shakti. For all beings including deities, the cycle of one day and night is based on 21,600 breaths and Sadasiva's breaths are without count, so He is undecaying. Shiva instructed them to continue their activities using these Gunas.

Vishnu, understanding and respecting Shiva's words, promised to always meditate on Shiva, and to act according to his directions, and also vowed that anyone who censures Shiva will be doomed to hell and those who are devoted to Shiva will be his favorites. He also expressed that his own greatness was enhanced by Shiva and that if he ever fell short, then he should be excused. Upon hearing this, Shiva assures them that they would be excused lovingly. Shiva lovingly stroked their bodies and gave them instructions on various rituals and gave them many blessings. Then, he vanished right in front of them. From that time on, the practice of worshipping the Linga was established. Shiva, present in the Linga, grants worldly pleasures and liberation, and the goddess is its base. The Linga is Shiva himself, and all the universe merges into it.

It's said that anyone who reads the stories of the Linga near a Linga will become like Shiva in six months. Also, any activity done near a Linga brings immense blessings.

This chapter explains the greatness of Shiva, his compassion, and how devotion to him and the worship of his Linga can bring about worldly pleasures and ultimate liberation. It also highlights the unity of Vishnu, Brahma, and Shiva, all working for the benefit of the world.

Chapter Eleven

(THE SIMPLE GUIDE TO WORSHIPING SHIVA)

The chapter begins with a group of wise sages expressing their gratitude to Suta, a disciple of Vyasa, for sharing the sacred stories of Shiva. They acknowledge the divine power of the Shiva lingam and its ability to remove suffering. The sages then ask Suta to explain how to worship Shiva in a way that pleases Him, referencing a conversation between Brahma and Narada, because they want to know how they should worship Shiva.

Suta acknowledges the importance of the question and shares that the knowledge of Shiva's worship is a profound secret. He explains that he will share the teachings to the best of his ability, based on what he has learned. Suta clarifies the lineage of this knowledge, stating that Vyasa had asked the same question to Sanatkumara, Upamanyu learned it from Sanatkumara, and Vyasa received the knowledge from Upamanyu which was then shared with him. He states that he will explain it the same way Brahma explained it to Narada.

Brahma, speaking to Narada, explains that while a detailed explanation of Shiva worship would be incredibly lengthy, he will share a concise method. He emphasizes that devoted worship of Shiva fulfills all desires. Brahma says that poverty, sickness, enemies, and sins plague those who do not worship Shiva. Worshipping Shiva eradicates all suffering, brings happiness, and leads to salvation. He also states that all humans irrespective of caste can worship Shiva to fulfill their desires.

Brahma then details the steps of worship. It starts before sunrise with remembering one's teacher and Shiva, meditating on Hari, remembering deities, and reciting a prayer to Shiva. Following this, one should clean the body and use earth for cleansing purposes after evacuating bowels in the south direction. The earth should be used based on caste. After cleaning, washing of hands and feet is important.

Brahma continues, stating that cleaning teeth with a twig of specific length based on caste is important, however, this should be avoided on certain holy days. The devotee should take a bath, dress in clean clothes, and perform their daily prayers in a quiet, isolated space. After this, they should prepare the space for worship, find a seat, and start the rituals.

He continues to explain the ritualistic set up before worship, arranging the pedestal for the lingam, or creating an eight-petaled lotus diagram and placing Shiva in the center. The devotee should then sit with all the worship materials around them. They should perform purification rituals like **Achamana**, **breath-holding exercises**, and **meditation**, in which they identify with Shiva to remove sins, visualizing Shiva's five faces, ten arms, ornaments, and tiger skin.

Brahma then explains the purification process with the use of holy water, reciting mantras and touching various parts of the body. Then, the preparation of the worship vessels for Padya, Arghya, and Achamana is stated. Nine different vessels should be used, with Darbha grass and cool water. Fragrant materials, such as roots of plants, sandal paste, and powders are mixed with the water in the vessels. Then Nandi, the bull is worshipped and Shiva is worshipped using scents, incense, and lamps.

Brahma goes on stating that the lingam is purified with mantras. The pedestal should be assigned with pranava and the eight petals are associated with eight achievements. The four quarters are associated with Avyakta, and three gunas. Lord Shiva should be invoked using various mantras. Then, Rudra should be worshipped using specific mantras, and Padya, Achamaniya and Arghya should be offered. The deity should then be bathed with water, and fragrant materials. Then with milk, curds, honey, and sugarcane juice, all accompanied with prayers. Then the deity is worshipped using ghee, and water is poured using mantras.

After the bathing, the water should be strained before using, and raw rice should be offered with sandalwood paste. Flowers, specifically white and rare flowers such as Apamarga, Karpura, Jati, Champaka, Kusa, Patala, Karavira, Mallika, Kamala (lotus), and Utpalas (lilies) should be offered to Shiva. Then water should be poured in a continuous stream. Different varieties of vessels can be used for this ritual bath and should be done using mantras for greatest benefit. He further adds that mantras can be committed to memory, spoken or read, including Rudra mantra, Nilarudra mantra, Sukla Yajurveda mantras, Atharva mantras, Santi mantras, Maruta mantras, etc. Water should be offered 1000 or 108 times.

Brahma explains that sandalwood paste, flowers, and sweet smelling cloves should be offered with mantras to Shiva. He goes on to explain the true nature of the Shiva lingam - pure, unending, the cause of the universe, beyond the reach of even Brahma, Vishnu, and other gods, incomprehensible to those who don't know the Vedas, without beginning, middle, or end, a cure for all ills, and known as Siva Tattva. He emphasizes that the lingam should be worshipped with the Pranava mantra and with incense, lamps, food offerings (naivedyas), betel leaves, and waving of lights (nirajana). Prayers, prostrations, and offerings of flowers at the foot of the lingam should be made. The devotee should kneel and pray with utmost devotion.

Brahma says, that the devotee should then stand with flowers in their hand and pray, seeking forgiveness for any mistakes made during the worship and ask for the blessings of Shiva. After praying, the flowers are offered to the lingam. Following this, benediction rituals, prayers for forgiveness, and Achamana are performed. The devotee should again pray, with a focus on devotion to Shiva in every birth and stating that Shiva is their only refuge.

Brahma explains, after this prayer, the devotee should again pray to the lord loudly, perform namaskara with family, and feel happy. The devotee should then carry on their day as per convenience. He further states that those who consistently worship Shiva with devotion will achieve success in everything. Shiva will remove all their miseries, sorrows, and ailments quickly, and their happiness will increase every day, just like the waxing moon.

Finally Suta concludes his narration, mentioning he has told them the mode of worship of Shiva and then asks if they would like to hear anything else.

Chapter Twelve

(WHAT'S REALLY IMPORTANT IN SHIVA WORSHIP)

The chapter begins with Narada, who is speaking to his father Brahma, praising Brahma's devotion to Shiva. Narada requests Brahma to further clarify the essential aspects of Shiva worship. This sets the stage for a deeper dive into what truly matters in spiritual practice.

Brahma recounts an event where he gathered all the sages and gods. He lovingly suggested they go to the shore of the milk ocean to seek guidance on achieving lasting happiness. This sets the background for a revelation about the nature of worship.

Brahma explains that they all went to Lord Vishnu, bowed down, and prayed. Upon seeing them, Vishnu remembered Shiva and spoke. This introduces Vishnu as a key figure in clarifying the importance of Shiva worship.

Vishnu asks Brahma and the deities the reason for their visit. Brahma explained that the deities asked about whom should they worship regularly to remove their miseries. Vishnu replies that Shiva, the destroyer of miseries, should be worshipped by all who seek happiness. He explains that he and Brahma have already been told this by Shiva himself. He emphasizes the importance of consistent worship and states that those who abandon the worship of Shiva face destruction.

Vishnu emphasizes that the worship of the Shiva lingam is essential for sustenance and well-being for everyone, including gods, demons, and even Vishnu and Brahma themselves. He stresses that even a single moment spent without worshipping Shiva is a great loss and a foolish act. He clarifies that those who focus on Shiva will never face misery.

Vishnu continues stating that those who wish for material wealth, beautiful surroundings, healthy life, worldly and heavenly happiness, and ultimate salvation, should consistently worship Shiva through good deeds. Vishnu says that those who worship Shiva regularly and with devotion will achieve success and will not be affected by sins.

Brahma explains that the gods requested Vishnu to provide them with Shiva lingams so that they may achieve their desires. Vishnu then directed Vishwakarma to create Shiva lingams. Vishwakarma created various lingams made of different materials, and distributed them to the gods based on their status. Brahma states that he will now share those with Narada.

Brahma then lists the different gods and what type of lingams they received: Indra (ruby), Kubera (gold), Dharma (yellow stone), Varuna (dark blue), Vishnu (sapphire), Brahma (gold), the Visvedevas and Vasus (silver), the Asvini devas (bronze and earth), Lakshmi (crystal), the Adityas (copper), the Moon (pearl), and Agni (diamond). He also lists other important figures and the materials of their lingams. He lists Brahmins (earth), Maya (sandalwood), Shesha Naga (coral), Goddesses (butter), Yogis (ash), Yakshas (curd), and Chaya (beaten flour). He also mentions that goddess Brahmani worships gem lingam, and Bana and others worship mercury lingam. These various materials highlight the diversity of devotion.

After distributing the lingams, Vishnu explained the proper way to worship Shiva to Brahma. Brahma then shared the method with the gods and sages. He then addressed the gods and sages by stating that human birth is rare, and birth in a good Brahmin family is even more rare. He said those who get such an auspicious life, should perform Shiva rites. He emphasizes that one should not transgress from their caste and do good deeds and charity as per their capacity.

Brahma then speaks about the importance of different forms of sacrifice, stating that penance is better than rituals, chanting is better than penance, and meditation is best. He explains that through meditation one is able to see God. He emphasizes that Shiva is always near someone who meditates. He also mentions that those who have attained true knowledge do not need rituals as they are beyond good and evil.

Brahma states that the Shiva lingam present in the hearts of yogis is pure and unblemished. He emphasizes that the lingam can be internal (subtle) and external (gross). Those who are engaged in rituals, worship the gross lingam as they are not able to steady their minds. He explains that until someone masters their inner mind, they should worship the gross lingam. He states that, to a learned person the subtle lingam is the same as the gross lingam is to a novice.

Brahma explains that everything in the universe, whether it appears with form or without, is a form of Shiva, and this should always be kept in mind. He explains that even those who have not attained perfect knowledge are not without their merit. He states that even if a wise person continues to live a householder's life, they are not bound by the rules and restrictions of such a life.

Brahma states that until someone attains perfect knowledge they should continue the worship of Shiva as well as perform their duties. He also explains that the idols are important for those who haven't attained true knowledge as it helps them focus on the formless Shiva. The idol helps the seeker attain the Nirguna Shiva through the Saguna. He says that without an idol, offerings like scents and flowers are of no use. He says that if a seeker does not worship an idol before attaining perfect knowledge, then downfall is sure.

Brahma emphasizes that one should perform their duties and worship with devotion. He states that without worship, sins cannot be removed. He explains that when the body is cleansed with proper worship, the dye of knowledge can stick to it, helping one gain true knowledge. He explains that devotion is the root of knowledge and a good teacher is the root of devotion, and that good teachers are found through good company.

Brahma explains that knowledge leads to realization of Brahman and when this happens differentiations end, and so does suffering. He says that those who are free from suffering become one with Shiva. He explains that those who have attained true knowledge are beyond do's and don'ts. He states that such people are rare, and even their mere presence can remove sins. He states that such people are higher than holy places and idols and that they purify all with just their vision.

Brahma emphasizes that until one is a householder, they should worship deities with devotion. However, it is enough if one worships Shiva. He states that by propitiating Shiva all other gods are automatically worshipped. Therefore, one should worship Shiva for the good of all living beings and for the attainment of all desires.

Chapter Thirteen

(THE DIVINE RITUALS OF SHIVA WORSHIP)

Brahma begins by addressing the sages and gods, promising to share the best way to worship Shiva, which will lead to happiness and the fulfillment of all desires. This sets the tone for a detailed explanation of the rituals involved in Shiva worship.

Brahma explains that the day should start before dawn, during Brahma Muhurta, by remembering Shiva and his consort. The devotee should join their palms, bow their head, and offer prayers, asking Shiva to awaken and bless the universe. They should acknowledge their weaknesses and express that all their actions are guided by Shiva. This highlights the importance of devotion and surrendering to a higher power.

Brahma continues that after prayers, one should remember their teacher and go out to answer the call of nature, in the south direction. The body should be cleaned with earth and water, then hands and feet should be washed, and the teeth should be cleaned before sunrise. One should gargle sixteen times. He then lists days where cleaning of teeth with twigs is prohibited. This emphasizes the importance of physical and spiritual purity.

Brahma explains that bathing should be done at a convenient time and place, not against local customs or the season. He lists times when hot water baths should be avoided. Oil baths are permissible according to custom or for scented oils but should be avoided on certain holy days. He explains that one should always face either the north or east while taking a bath.

Brahma states one should not wear other›s clothes during bath and that one should bathe in clean clothes. After the bath, one should offer water to gods, sages, and ancestors. He should then wear clean and dry clothes and perform Acamana. The devotee should then take their seat in a clean place, which is smeared with cow dung.

Brahma explains that the seat for worship can be made of wood or cloth, with diverse colors being ideal. A deer hide is also an acceptable option for seating and the individual should apply Tripundra using ashes, or water if ashes are not available. He emphasizes that prayers, penance, and charity should be done with the Tripundra applied on the forehead. Rudraksha beads are also to be worn. He then states that one should start the worship after daily routines are over.

Brahma states that one should perform Acamana (sipping of water) thrice or once saying that is Ganga water. They should have rice cooked with water, and other worship materials near them. He mentions that a vessel of Arghya should be brought, which contains water and scented raw rice grains. This vessel should be kept on the right shoulder. He then says one should remember the teacher, take permission for the worship, perform Samkalpa and start the worship of Shiva and his attendants.

Brahma explains that one should bow to and worship Ganesha, along with his consorts Siddhi and Buddhi, and should use saffron and other materials for this. Then Ganesha should be worshiped in the company of Kartikeya. After this, big-bellied Ganesha, who is the gatekeeper of the lord, and Goddess Sati and Girija should be worshiped. This step highlights the importance of seeking blessings from other deities before proceeding with Shiva worship.

Brahma explains that after offering sandalwood paste, saffron, incense, various lamps, and food to Shiva, one should bow down again. He says that one can worship a Shiva lingam made of clay, silver, metal or mercury at home, and if that is worshipped then all deities are worshiped. If it's made of clay, it should be properly installed. He says that householders should perform every rite per rules.

Brahma says that if worship is done in a temple, then guardians of the quarters should be worshiped. But at home, Shiva can be worshiped using a root mantra. He says there is no need to worship a gatekeeper at home. He states that the lingam he worships can be worshiped at home as everything is within it. He also states that at the time of worship, Shiva should be invoked along with his attendants.

Brahma explains that one should provide a seat near Shiva, face north, perform Acamana, wash hands and feet, and perform Pranayama ten times with the Mulamantra. Then one should perform five mystic Mudras. The worship should only be done after showing the Mudras. Then lamp should be shown and homage should be paid to the teacher.

Brahma continues by explaining that after this one should sit in a yogic pose (Padma, Bhadra, Uttana or Paryahka). He mentions that if the worship is done at home, the rules are not binding. He states that after the worship, one should wash the lingam with water from the Arghya vessel after having arranged the materials mindfully.

Brahma then provides a detailed mantra for invoking Shiva, including his form, qualities, and attendants. He says after this meditation, the seat should be arranged and worship should begin with names ending in the dative case. He states that Padya and Arghya should be offered to Shiva. Acamana should be offered and Shiva should be bathed with five materials (milk, curds, honey, etc.). Offerings should be made with Vedic mantras or names ending in dative case.

Brahma continues that desirable materials should be offered to Shiva. After that Varuna Snana (ceremonial ablution) should be performed. Fragrant sandalwood paste should be applied and the water should be poured over Shiva in a continuous stream. Water ablutions should be made with Vedic mantras or the six-syllable mantra. After that, the lingam should be wiped with a cloth and Acamana and cloths should be dedicated. Gingelly seeds, barley grains, wheat, green gram, or black gram should be offered to Shiva along with flowers to the five faced lord.

Brahma then states various flowers like lotuses, roses, Sankha, Kusa flowers, Dhatturas, Mandaras grown in a wooden vessel, holy basil leaves, or Bilva leaves can be offered. He emphasizes the devotion, and also explains that if other flowers are not available, Bilva leaves can be used exclusively for the worship of Shiva. After this scented powders, sweet smelling oils etc should be offered. Then incense, Guggulu and Aguru should be offered.

Brahma explains that after offering incense, a ghee lamp should be offered to Shiva. Then face should be wiped with a cloth. Then Arghya should be offered with the mantra "O Siva, give us good features, good fame, and good enjoyment of pleasures. Taking this Arghya give us the pleasures of the world and salvation. Obeisance be to Thee." Then various kinds of food offerings should be offered. Acamana should be performed immediately and betel leaves should be offered with all necessary ingredients. Arartika should be performed with a lamp with five wicks. He explains how light should be waved using the five wicked lamp.

Brahma says then the devotee should meditate and repeat the mantras and eulogise Shiva. He explains that they should circumambulate the lingam, perform prostration with eight limbs and then offer flowers with devotion saying the mantra- "O Siva, whatever I have done by way of worship etc. with or without sufficient knowledge for Siva the great lord, in order to secure His satisfaction shall be fruitful by your grace. O Mpja, I belong to you. My vital airs are fixed in you. My mind is always concentrated in you. O Gauri'a, O lord of goblins, be pleased with me. Those who stagger and falter on the ground are supported by the ground alone. O lord, those who have offended you shall find in you alone as their refuge".

Brahma states that after the prayers, the devotee should bid farewell to Shiva, requesting him to return to his abode in their hearts and apply the holy water on their head. He concludes that he has completely explained the method of Shiva worship that leads to both worldly pleasures and salvation, and asks if there is anything else they wish to hear.

Chapter Fourteen

(THE POWER OF FLOWERS AND OFFERINGS IN SHIVA WORSHIP)

The sages, led by Saunaka, asked Suta about the benefits of worshipping Lord Shiva with different offerings. Suta explained, as told by Brahma to Narada, that worshipping Shiva with various flowers, leaves, and grains fulfills desires and grants spiritual progress.

For instance, lotus petals and Bilva leaves bring wealth, while offerings like Dhattura flowers ensure long life or sons. Worship with Tulasi leaves grants both worldly pleasures and salvation, while using Japa flowers destroys enemies.

Brahma emphasized that the sincerity of the devotee is more important than the materials used. Performing rituals like offering incense, lamps, food, and chanting mantras enhances the effects. For seekers of liberation, repeated chanting of Shiva's mantras, such as the Mrityunjaya mantra, is highly beneficial. Worship with specific grains or pulses, such as barley or sesame, is prescribed for different desires, including prosperity, happiness, and overcoming enemies.

Dhara worship, where water or other liquids are poured continuously over the Shiva Linga while chanting mantras, is highlighted as powerful for curing ailments, improving intellect, and fulfilling wishes. Using substances like ghee, milk, or honey during Dhara worship is said to bestow specific benefits, such as family prosperity or wealth.

Suta concluded that sincere worship of Shiva, accompanied by rituals like feeding Brahmins and performing the Prajapatya rites, leads to worldly happiness, spiritual growth, and ultimately liberation. Those who worship with devotion are blessed to enjoy the eternal presence of Lord Shiva in his divine abode.

Chapter Fifteen

(THE EMERGENCE OF RUDRA AND THE START OF CREATION)

Narada praises Brahma for sharing the stories of Shiva and asks him to describe what happened after Shiva vanished and how creation began.

Brahma agrees and explains that after Shiva disappeared, he and Vishnu happily withdrew their forms of Swan and Boar, ready to create and sustain the world.

Narada asks why Brahma and Vishnu took the forms of a Swan and Boar. Suta narrates that Brahma explains, remembering Shiva's lotus feet.

Brahma explains to Narada that the swan can travel upwards and discern real from unreal, representing his role as creator. However, he failed to know Shiva's true form and that knowledge cannot come while in creation. Vishnu took the form of a boar to travel downwards and start a new generation, named Varaha.

After Shiva vanished, Brahma contemplated creation and was guided by Vishnu. Vishnu established Vaikuntha, and Brahma, remembering Shiva and Vishnu, offered water offering that turned into a cosmic egg. He became confused and did penance for twelve years.

Vishnu appeared and said that by Shiva's favor, he could grant Brahma anything. Brahma asked Vishnu to give consciousness to the unconsious cosmic egg that had arisen from Shiva's power.

Vishnu, following Shiva's guidance, entered the cosmic egg, filling it with his forms and touched everywhere, giving it consciousness. Vishnu shone as the great being of the seven worlds, and Shiva created Kailasa. Brahma resides in Satyaloka.

The five illusions appeared before Brahma as he desired to create, followed by immobile beings. This creation lacked aspiration. Then came the divine creation, but they too lacked aspiration. The human creation came next, which was an aspirant. And then came the creation of the elements. These six types of creations are collectively called Vaikrita.

Brahma created three more forms from Prakriti - the cosmic intellect, subtle elements, and transformations. He also mentions the ninth creation called Kaumara Sarga, and then Brahminical Creation which included Sanaka and others.

Sanaka and his mental sons, refused to engage in creation and instead meditated on Shiva, retorting when Brahma commanded them. Furious, Brahma shed tears, and Vishnu guided him to perform Shiva's penance.

During penance, Shiva appeared as Ardhanarishvara (half-man, half-woman) between Brahma's eyebrows and nose. Brahma asked him to create the subjects.

Lord Rudra responded he would not create beings bound by suffering, but he would guide them with knowledge. Brahma was to create the suffering subjects, free from illusion. Shiva vanished with his attendants, leaving Brahma to continue creation.

Chapter Sixteen

(HOW THE UNIVERSE WAS CREATED BY BRAHMA)

This chapter explains how Brahma created the universe, all thanks to Shiva. Brahma tells Narada that after creating the basic elements, he made the grosser ones like ether, wind, fire, water, and earth. He fashioned mountains, seas, trees, and the different time cycles. Still not satisfied, Brahma meditated on Shiva and Amba, which led him to create the first aspirants, or great sages.

He then created Marici from his eyes, Bhrigu from his heart, Angiras from his head, Pulaha from his vital breath, Pulastya from Udana, Vasishta from Samana, Kratu from Apana, Atri from his ears, Daksha from Prana, you from my lap, Kardama from my shadow and finally Dharma from his conception. Through Shiva's grace, he was finally pleased with the creation of these great sadhakas.

Then Dharma transformed into Manu who helped him with creation. Following this, Brahma created countless sons, Devas (gods), and Asuras (demons) from different parts of his body. Inspired by Shiva within him, Brahma split himself into a male and female form. The male form was Swayambhuva Manu and the female was Satarupa. Manu married Satarupa and they created beings through intercourse, resulting in sons Priyavrata and Uttanapada, and three daughters Akuti, Devahuti, and Prasuti. These daughters were married off and their descendants populated the world.

Further, Daksha had sixty daughters, ten given to Dharma, twenty-seven to the Moon, thirteen to Kasyapa and the others were given to the other sages. The children of these daughters spread throughout the three worlds. This filled the space between Patala and Satyaloka and the whole cosmic egg was filled according to Shiva's will.

Sati, the daughter of Daksha, was kept safe by Rudra, who held her on the tip of his trident during her period of penance. Though Shiva himself was her original creator, she later took birth through Daksha to participate in worldly affairs. The Lord's divine pastimes were undertaken to guide and uplift his devotees.

Then at the request of the gods, Shiva incarnated her as Parvati. By doing rigorous penance, Parvati obtained Shiva as her husband. She became known by various names like Kali, Chandika, and Durga, each name having specific qualities and effects.

Brahma also explains how Shiva manifests in three ways: Vishnu (from his left), Brahma (from his right), and Rudra (from his heart), each representing the three Gunas - Sattva, Rajas, and Tamas respectively for the workings of the world.

Finally, Brahma declares that Shiva is the supreme Brahman and the three deities (Vishnu, Brahma, Rudra) are his manifestations according to the difference in the attributes. Rudra is the perfect and complete incarnation of Shiva who resides in the majestic Kailasa.

Chapter Seventeen

(THE STORY OF GUNANIDHI)

This chapter tells the story of Gunanidhi, a man whose life took a turn from virtue to vice. Suta explains that after hearing Brahma's creation story, Narada asked about Shiva's time in Kailasa with Kubera. Brahma then starts narrating the story of Gunanidhi. In Kampilya city lived a respected Brahmin named Yajnadatta, an expert in sacrifices, Vedas and Vedanta. He had a son, Gunanidhi, who was handsome and well-versed in scriptures initially but he secretly became addicted to gambling.

Gunanidhi would take money from his mother to give to fellow gamblers. He abandoned Brahmin customs, avoided prayers, spoke ill of Vedas, devas, and Brahmins. His mother tried to guide him towards the right path, reminding him of his family's tradition and his duties. She also tried to protect her son by lying to her husband. She told him that Gunanidhi is going out for studies when he is actually going out to gamble. Even after Gunanidhi's marriage, she continued to advise him to shun bad company and follow his father's good example.

Despite his mother's advice, Gunanidhi continued his bad habits, even stealing valuable items from home to pay his gambling debts. One day, his father saw a ring he had given to his wife in the hands of a gambler, who confessed that Gunanidhi had given it to him. When Yajnadatta confronted his wife about the missing ring and other valuable items, she lied and made up an excuse. The wife had been lying so far, saying that their son was studying Vedas when he was actually gambling. Yajnadatta was furious. He declared that he would marry again since he was now childless after his son's actions. Yajnadatta performed rites for a dead person (Gunanidhi), and married another woman on the same day as he would rather be childless than have a wicked son.

Chapter Eighteen

(GUNANIDHI'S PATH TO REDEMPTION)

This chapter tells the story of how Gunanidhi, the son of Yajnadatta, went from a life of vice to becoming a beloved devotee of Shiva. Brahma explains that after being disowned by his father, Gunanidhi was filled with regret. He wandered aimlessly, feeling lost and abandoned. He reflected on his poor choices, acknowledging his lack of education, wealth, and good character. As the sun set, he found himself near a Shiva temple, where he saw a group of devotees bringing offerings for the night.

Driven by hunger, Gunanidhi hoped to steal the food offered to Shiva. He waited until the devotees fell asleep, then entered the temple. The lamp was dim, so he tore a piece of cloth from his garment to use as a wick, brightening the light so he could see the sweets. As he was leaving, he was caught by the watchmen and was killed. The messengers of Yama, the god of death, came to take Gunanidhi but the attendants of Shiva arrived to take him to Sivaloka. They said Gunanidhi has burnt away his sins. The messengers of Yama argued but the attendants of Shiva explained that even though Gunanidhi had bad intention his actions have saved him. By adding to the lamp, he prevented its shadow from falling on the Shiva linga, thus making it very auspicious. He also heard the names of Shiva, witnessed his worship, and his mind was focused.

The attendants of Shiva take Gunanidhi to Sivaloka. They also declared that Gunanidhi will be reborn as a king in Kalinga. Following this discussion, the emissaries of Yama returned to his abode. Yama then instructed his servants to avoid bringing to him those who wear the mark of Tripundra, those who apply ash, those who appear in garb of Shiva, those who wear Rudraksha beads, and all who imitate Shiva.

Gunanidhi enjoyed life in Sivaloka, serving Shiva and Parvati, and was then reborn as King Dama of Kalinga. King Dama, who was a devoted follower of Shiva, made sure that lamps were always burning in Shiva temples throughout his kingdom. Because of the power of good deeds he did in his past life he then went on to become the lord of Alaka. The story shows that even small acts of service to Shiva bear significant fruit, and encourages devotion.

Chapter Nineteen

(THE FRIENDSHIP OF SHIVA AND KUBERA)

This chapter describes how Kubera, the god of wealth, became a close friend of Shiva. Brahma narrates that in the Padma Kalpa, he created Pulastya, whose son Visravas had a son named Vaisravana (later known as Kubera). Through intense penance to Shiva, he had attained Alaka city.

In the following Meghavahana Kalpa, Gunanidhi (now known as Srida), the son of Yajnadatta, continued his devotion to Shiva. Understanding the merit of illuminating Shiva's temple with lamps, Srida reached Kashi, where he focused his mind on Shiva. For two hundred thousand years, he engaged in extreme penance, free from worldly desires and concentrating only on Shiva, worshipping the linga with pure thoughts.

Pleased with his devotion, Shiva, along with Parvati, appeared before Srida. Shiva offered him a boon, but Srida asked only for the ability to see Shiva's feet. Shiva touched him, granting him divine vision. When he opened his eyes, he first saw Parvati, admiring her beauty, love, and good fortune. However, his left eye burst upon seeing her.

Parvati took it as jealousy and complained to Shiva, but Shiva said he is describing her penance, glory and devotion and is not looking with jealousy. Shiva, delighted by Srida's devotion, granted him the boon of becoming the lord of treasures, the king of Yakshas and other celestial beings, and the giver of wealth. He promised to remain close to Alaka, strengthening their friendship. Shiva then introduced Parvati to Srida, calling Srida as her own son.

Parvati blessed Srida that his devotion to Shiva will remain forever. She also said he will be called Kubera for looking jealously at her and his left eye will be yellow, Ekapinga.After blessing Kubera, Shiva and Parvati returned to their abode. Thus, Kubera became Shiva's friend and his city of Alaka was very near Shiva's abode, Kailasa.

Chapter Twenty

(SHIVA'S ARRIVAL AT KAILASA)

This chapter narrates Shiva's journey to Kailasa and his establishment there, solidifying his friendship with Kubera. Brahma explains that after granting Kubera the lordship of treasures, Shiva returned to his abode and considered his next actions. He decided that Rudra, his manifestation, would take the form to go to Kailasa, as it was also the abode of Guhyakas. Rudra is his perfect form, worthy of worship by Vishnu, Brahma, and all. Shiva wished to stay near Kubera and practice penance as his friend.

Rudra, wanting to fulfill Shiva's wish, sounded his divine drum, whose resonating sound spread throughout the three worlds, calling everyone to his presence. Vishnu, Brahma, deities, sages, and various celestial beings came to see him.

Brahma then lists the names and numbers of the Ganas (Shiva's attendants) who came to join him. The Ganas are described as powerful, with many arms, matted hair, and adorned with celestial ornaments.

Shiva, surrounded by his followers, then went to Kailasa. Kubera greeted him with great respect, worshipping him with various gifts and also worshipping Vishnu and the other deities and Ganas.

Pleased with Kubera's devotion, Shiva embraced him and kissed him on the head. He then ordered Vishwakarma to build his and his followers residences on the mountain. Vishwakarma immediately carried out his orders.

At the request of Vishnu, Shiva then entered his new residence at an auspicious hour after blessing Kubera. Vishnu, other deities, sages, and Siddhas celebrated Shiva's coronation with festivities. Celestial damsels danced and sang with joy. Everyone rejoiced, shouting "victory" and "honour."

Seated on his throne, Shiva was served by Vishnu and others. Deities praised Shiva and he granted their wishes. Shiva then asked Brahma and Vishnu to return to their abodes. He then embraced Kubera once again, assuring him of his friendship and help.

Shiva stayed at Kailasa with his Ganas, practicing yoga, meditating, and engaging in divine sports. He spent time without his divine consort and later married Sati.

RUDRA SAMHITA SECTION II: NARRATIVE OF SATI

Chapter One

(THE STORY OF SATI AND HER REBIRTH AS PARVATI)

The sage Narada asks Brahma to share more stories about Shiva and Parvati. Brahma, pleased with Narada's devotion, agrees and begins by recounting a past incident where he, overcome by desire, offended Shiva. Realizing his mistake, Brahma, along with his sons, tried to trick Shiva, but failed, being deluded by Shiva's Maya. Then, influenced by Vishnu, Brahma decided to win Shiva over. He arranged for Shakti to be born as his son Daksha's daughter. She was named Sati. Sati grew up to marry Shiva.

Later, a feud developed between Sati's father, Daksha, and Shiva. Daksha, arrogant and still under the influence of Maya, organized a grand sacrifice but intentionally excluded Shiva and Sati. Sati, despite not being invited, went to her father's yajna, with Shiva's reluctant permission. There, she was insulted by her father and saw that Shiva was deliberately left out. Unable to bear the disrespect towards her husband, Sati immolated herself, abandoning her body in the fire of Yajna.

Virabhadra, following Shiva's orders, led an army of warriors to Daksha's sacrifice, wreaking havoc. He defeated the Devas, including Vishnu and ultimately beheaded Daksha (later his head was replaced by a goat head). He completely destroyed the sacrifice. After completing the destruction, Virabhadra returned to Shiva. The Gods, seeing Shiva's anger, pleaded with him, singing praises to soothe his wrath. Shiva, being compassionate, was moved by their prayers. He revived Daksha and restarted the sacrifice, where he himself was properly honored.

The flame that arose from Sati's immolated body fell on a mountain and became a sacred place of pilgrimage known as Jvalamukhi.

Later, Sati was reborn as Parvati, the daughter of Himalaya. She performed intense penance and, through her devotion, was finally reunited with Shiva as his wife. Brahma concluded by saying that whoever hears this story will be freed from their sins.

Chapter Two

(THE BIRTH OF KAMADEVA, THE GOD OF LOVE)

Suta, speaking to the sages, narrates how Narada again requests Brahma for more stories about Shiva and Sati. Narada is particularly interested in Sati's birth, marriage, death, and rebirth as Parvati. Brahma agrees to tell the story, mentioning that he initially heard it from Vishnu. He begins by describing the time before Shiva manifested in form. When Shiva did manifest with Shakti, Vishnu was born from his left side, Brahma from the right side, and Rudra (Shiva) from his heart.

This trinity manifested to look after the cosmos. Brahma then describes how after creating various beings, including the Prajapatis like Daksha, he developed a sense of pride.

From Brahma's mind, a beautiful woman named Sandhya was born. Her beauty captivated everyone, including Brahma and his sons. While thinking about her, another being manifested – a handsome man with golden skin, broad chest, and captivating eyes. He had a bow and five flower arrows. He was Kamadeva, the god of love.

Kamadeva asked Brahma about his purpose, his position, and who his wife would be. Brahma, captivated himself, explained that Kamadeva's role was to make everyone fall in love, including the gods, humans and all other living beings. He said that Kamadeva's flower arrows would ensure that all creatures feel desire, thus driving creation.

Brahma declared that even he, Vishnu, and Shiva himself would not be immune to Kamadeva's power. He assigned Kamadeva to the task of facilitating creation through love. After saying this, Brahma looked at his sons and sat back down on his lotus seat.

Chapter Three

(KAMADEVA'S CURSE AND BLESSING)

Brahma continues the story, explaining that his sons, the sages, named the newly born Kamadeva with names like Manmatha, Kama, Madana, Darpaka, and Kandarpa, meaning one who agitates minds, the god of love, one who causes elation and proud.

Daksha selected Sandhya as Kama's wife. Kamadeva then decided to test his powers, and he shot his five flower arrows (delighting, appealing, deluding, withering and killing) at Brahma and the sages. This made them all lustful and caused them to stare at Sandhya with inappropriate desire, making them loose control. Dharma, one of Brahma's sons, witnessed this and, feeling distressed, prayed to Lord Shiva for protection.

Shiva appeared, laughing at Brahma and the sages for succumbing to desire. He reminded them that they should be ashamed to look at their daughter/sister with lust.

Shiva then scolded Kama for misusing his powers. Ashamed, Brahma and others regained their senses. From Brahma's sweat, many manes (ancestral spirits) were born, along with a woman named Rati from Daksha's sweat.

Angered by the situation, Brahma cursed Kamadeva. He declared that Kama would be burnt to ashes by Shiva's third eye for his arrogance. Kamadeva, frightened, begged for mercy, arguing that he was only fulfilling his assigned task and following Brahma's words, testing them all, including Brahma himself. Brahma, having calmed down, modified the curse, saying that while Shiva would indeed burn Kama to ashes, Kama would be reborn when Shiva took a wife. After saying this Brahma disappeared. Kamadeva and all others went back to their respective abodes, relieved but also mindful of the fate of Kama.

Chapter Four

(THE MARRIAGE OF KAMADEVA AND RATI)

Narada asks Brahma what happened after Shiva left and Brahma vanished. Brahma explains that Daksha remembered Brahma's words and offered Rati, the woman born from his sweat, to Kamadeva as his wife.

Daksha said that Rati was born of his body, beautiful, and well-suited for Kamadeva. He ensured that she would be his constant companion.

Brahma said that Kamadeva happily married Rati and was instantly enchanted by her beauty. He became so captivated that he was consumed by the pleasures of love and forgot all about Brahma's curse. He found her more beautiful than anything he knew.

Brahma describes Rati's beauty in detail, highlighting her features like her eyebrows that resembled his own bow, her swift glances, her fragrant breath, her moon-like face, her breasts that looked like golden lotus buds, her slender waist, and her reddish feet.

He said she had a disc and a lotus in her hand and that she was like Goddess Lakshmi herself. She also adorned 12 types of ornaments and knew 16 amorous gestures. He compared her to the Ganga flowing down a snowy mountain. She had a deep navel like a deep eddy.

Kamadeva was so entranced that he forgot his own bow and arrows, lost in her charm. He accepted her just as Vishnu accepted Lakshmi. Great festivities followed their marriage, and Daksha was delighted to see them happy. Kamadeva, completely deluded by his joy, completely forgot about Brahma's curse. Rati, too, was overjoyed to find such a wonderful husband. They rejoiced together.

Chapter Five

(THE STORY OF SANDHYA'S PENANCE AND REBIRTH)

Narada, pleased with Brahma's stories, asks about Sandhya's fate. He wants to know what happened to her after Kamadeva's marriage, where she went, and who she married.

Brahma then narrates Sandhya's story: Sandhya, feeling guilty and distressed after the incident where Brahma and the sages lusted after her, resolved to do penance to purify herself and set new limits about lust at the time of birth. She recognized that her own mind had been corrupted with lust, and that she needed to make amends. She decided that the body that had caused so much trouble was not worthy.

Sandhya went to the Candrabhaga mountain to perform penance. Brahma, aware of her actions, sent his son, the sage Vasistha, to guide her. Brahma asked Vasistha to disguise himself so Sandhya would not be embarrassed to see him and to explain how she could achieve her goal. Vasistha found her near a beautiful lake. He asked her why she was there and what she intended to do. Sandhya, after bowing to him, told him she had come to perform penance. She also mentioned that she had witnessed all that has happened so she needs guidance on how to do the penance.

Vasistha, disguised as a sage, told her to meditate on Shiva and gave her a mantra: **"Om Namah Samkaraya Om."** He instructed her to observe silence during the penance, take a bath silently, worship Shiva silently, and only consume water during the first two periods of the day and to fast on the third period. She needed to continue this process until the end of the penance and to perform the rites at the end of each period. Vasistha assured her that this penance would purify her, and if Shiva was pleased, he would grant her wishes. After instructing her, Vasistha vanished.

Chapter Six

(SANDHYA'S DEVOTION, DIVINE BOONS, AND DESTINY)

Brahma continues his narration, explaining the profound penance undertaken by Sandhya. After Sage Vasistha instructed her on the proper rites, Sandhya began her intense spiritual practice on the banks of the Brhallohita lake. She adopted the attire of a seeker and meditated deeply upon Lord Shiva, using the mantra given to her. This continued for four long Yugas, showing her unwavering dedication.

Impressed by her devotion, Lord Shiva revealed himself to Sandhya — appearing both within her heart, in the outside world and also in heaven. He took the form upon which she was meditating. Overwhelmed, Sandhya closed her eyes in reverence. Shiva then blessed her with divine wisdom, divine speech, and divine sight. With these new gifts, Sandhya opened her eyes and composed a beautiful hymn praising Shiva's formless and formful aspects.

In her hymn, Sandhya expressed her understanding of Shiva as the ultimate reality, beyond description or form. She recognized him as the creator, preserver, and destroyer. She also praised his pure, luminous nature and sought his grace. Lord Shiva, pleased by her devotion, declared that he was delighted with her penance and asked her to choose her boons.

Sandhya humbly requested several boons: First, that no being should be born with lust at the time of their birth. Second, that no other woman should be as famous as her for her purity. She also wished that her creations would never be degraded by lust. Additionally, she asked that her husband be a friend with a pure mind, and that anyone who looked upon her with lust would become impotent.

Lord Shiva, touched by her earnestness and the purity of her requests, granted all her boons. He declared that lust would only arise later in life and that she would become an example of chastity. He also revealed that any man other than her husband who looked at her lustfully would indeed lose his potency and be weak. He also confirmed that her husband would be noble and that they would be together for seven Kalpas.

Furthermore, Shiva informed Sandhya that her destiny was to cast off her body in the sacrificial fire of the sage Medhatithi. He told her that he had ordained this for his own purpose and that she was pure and free from sin. She would be reborn as Medhatithi's fire-born daughter, Arundhati. She needed to think of her chosen husband while giving her body to the fire. Shiva also narrated a past incident about Daksha's daughters and the moon's curse and how river Chandrabhaga was created for the same purpose. He told her that she was not aware of the Gods' arrival near her while she was deep in penance and that Medhatithi was now present there. He described Medhatithi as an unparalleled sage who had now started a great sacrifice. Shiva instructed her to go to Medhatithi's sacrifice, fulfill her destiny, and then vanished, leaving Sandhya to follow the path he had revealed.

Chapter Seven

(ARUNDHATI'S BIRTH AND MARRIAGE TO VASISTHA)

Brahma continues to narrate Sandhya's story. After Shiva granted her the boons and disappeared, Sandhya went to the place where the sage Medhatithi was performing his sacrifice. Thanks to Shiva's grace, she entered the sacrificial hall unseen. Remembering the brahmin boy who had taught her the penance, she knew he was Vasistha. She meditated on him as her future husband and entered the blazing sacrificial fire, delighted that she could do so by Shiva's favor.

Sandhya's body turned into a sacrificial offering. At Shiva's direction, the fire god sent her essence to the sun, who divided it into two. The upper half became the Pratah Sandhya (dawn) and the lower half became the Sayamsandhya (dusk) – these times are always pleasing to gods and manes. Shiva created a new body for her using her life force.

At the end of the sacrifice, Medhatithi found a beautiful girl in the sacrificial pit. She was shining like gold. He took her up with great joy, and bathed her, then holding her in his lap. He named her Arundhati, meaning "one who does not hinder sacred rites." She grew up in the hermitage, Tapasaranya, near the Candrabhaga River.

When she turned five, she was known for her good qualities and had sanctified the river and the surrounding area. Brahma, Vishnu, and Shiva arranged her marriage with Vasistha, the same sage who had taught her the penance, and who was also Brahma's son. Great festivities followed their wedding, and the gods and sages were very happy.

From the water that dripped from the hands of Brahma, Vishnu, and Shiva during the marriage ceremony, seven sacred rivers, including Sipra, began to flow. Arundhati, the greatest of chaste women, shined even brighter after marrying Vasistha and became the mother of auspicious sons like Shakti. Brahma concluded that whoever hears this sacred story would have all their desires fulfilled.

Chapter Eight

(THE BIRTH OF VASANTA: SPRING'S ARRIVAL)

The chapter begins with Narada asking Brahma to narrate more tales of Shiva. Suta, the narrator, explains that Brahma, still disturbed by Shiva's words, is happy to oblige. Brahma, reveals to Narada how he initially felt resentful towards Shiva for not being interested in marriage. He explains to Narada that because he was deluded by Shiva's Maya, he hatched a plan to make Shiva desire a wife.

Brahma gathers his sons, including Daksha and asks them for help in making Shiva desire a wife. He tells them he felt insulted by Shiva's lack of interest in worldly matters. Brahma believes that the only way to achieve peace of mind is to get Shiva to marry and be bound by worldly desires. He calls upon Kama, the god of love and his wife Rati to help in this task. Brahma motivates Kama and Rati, he assures them that by making Shiva fall in love, Kama will achieve his purpose. Kama says that his primary weapon is a woman and asks Brahma to create a suitable maiden.

Brahma then ponders over who could enchant Shiva, and as he sighs deeply, Vasanta, the personification of spring, is born.

Vasanta is beautiful, with eyes like lotuses, a face like the moon, and a majestic gait. Brahma announces to Kama that Vasanta will be his constant companion and help him in his task, just as the wind helps fire, Vasanta will help Kama in his task of arousing desire. Spring will help Kama in his task. Brahma names him Vasanta and tells him that he will be always with Kama to help him enchant people. Brahma also declares that feminine arts, will be Rati's friends.

Finally, Brahma declares that he will create the perfect woman to captivate Shiva. Kama, delighted, bows down to Brahma, Daksha and other sages, and sets off with his wife Rati, and Vasanta to find Shiva.

Chapter Nine

(KAMA'S FAILED ATTEMPTS AND THE BIRTH OF HIS TROOPS)

Brahma begins by narrating to Narada, the events that unfolded after Kama and Vasanta (spring) went to Shiva's abode. He explains that although Kama used all his seductive skills and spring made the environment very alluring, Shiva remained unaffected by all the charm.

Kama returns to Brahma, admitting his failure. He says that Shiva is a master of Yoga, making it impossible to charm him. Kama recounts all the efforts that he, Rati and Spring took to enchant Shiva- he sent fragrant winds, shot arrows of love, placed amorous birds before him, and spring bloomed all kinds of flowers. They used all means, but Lord Shiva was not even moved a little, Kama says to Brahma that he is unable to enchant Siva.

Kama explains to Brahma that not only were their attempts fruitless, but Shiva's intense gaze, like a raging fire, was so powerful that they couldn't even stand in his presence.

Upon hearing Kama's words and sighing in great distress, Brahma sighs deeply. From these deep sighs, emerge fierce beings, screaming "Kill!" and "Cut!". This sight stops Kama on his path. Kama, curious about these strange beings, asks Brahma who they are and what their purpose is.

Brahma explains that these beings are called "Maras," and they are Kama's attendants. Their role is to create confusion in the minds of those affected by Kama's arrows and create obstacles for those seeking wisdom. They will follow Kama and assist him always.

Kama, a little pleased, is again sent to Shiva, along with his new troop. Kama goes to Shiva again, but is still unable to enchant him, and returns again to Brahma disappointed. Kama tells Brahma that Shiva, was completely unmoved by their attempts, and because of Shiva's mercy his body wasn't reduced to ashes.

Kama states that if Brahma still wishes Shiva to marry, then he should take some other action but also with modesty. Finally, Kama returns with his troops to his own abode.

Chapter Ten

(BRAHMA AND VISHNU'S DISCUSSION)

The chapter starts with Narada praising Brahma for his devotion to Shiva. He asks Brahma what happened after Kama returned defeated. Brahma then recounts his feelings of frustration and disappointment upon the failure of his plan to make Shiva desire a wife. He says that he felt arrogant and confused.

Brahma, realizing his mistake, remembers Vishnu and calls out to him for guidance. Vishnu appears, adorned with his usual divine attributes, and asks Brahma why he has been summoned. Brahma explains his plan to enchant Shiva, and how it failed miserably. Vishnu is surprised at Brahma's attempt.

Brahma then confesses how, he was deluded by Vishnu's Maya, and how he developed anger towards Shiva when Shiva rebuked him for desiring his own daughter. He also expresses his belief that Shiva's marriage would end his sorrow.

Vishnu then gently rebukes Brahma for his foolishness. He clarifies that Shiva is not an ordinary being but the Supreme Brahman, the creator, preserver, and destroyer of all. Vishnu explains that Shiva is beyond qualities and that Brahma was wrong in thinking of Shiva as his son.

Vishnu then explains that Shiva is the supreme truth, formless and beyond description. He exists as Brahma, Vishnu, and Mahesh (Shiva), yet transcends these forms. He advises Brahma to seek refuge in Shiva and worship him. If Brahma wishes for Shiva to marry, Vishnu suggests that Brahma should do penance for Shiva and think of the Goddess. When Shiva takes an incarnation with the goddess, in their human form, they will marry.

Vishnu then reminds Brahma of the conversation they had with Shiva at the time of their birth. Shiva had told them that he would manifest as Rudra, a perfect form worthy of worship. Vishnu tells Brahma that Shiva, would also take three forms. Vishnu then talks about how Lakshmi, Saraswati and Sati will be wives of Vishnu, Brahma and Shiva respectively.

Finally, Vishnu tells Brahma that an effort should be made for the future incarnation of Sati. After this discourse, Vishnu disappears and Brahma, now enlightened, feels a sense of joy and his jealousy is completely gone.

Chapter Eleven

(DURGA'S HYMN AND A GRANTED BOON)

Narada asks Brahma what happened after Vishnu left. Brahma replies that he started to pray to Goddess Durga, the wife of Shiva, who is the source of all creation.

Brahma praises Durga as being omnipresent, eternal, and the mother of all gods. He describes her as the embodiment of knowledge, bliss, and the supreme soul. He prays to her, hoping that she will fulfill his wish, to make Shiva marry. After Brahma's prayers, Goddess Durga appears before him.

Brahma, filled with devotion, bows down and continues his praise. He explains that she is the essence of action and detachment, creation, and preservation. He also states she is present everywhere, even in the smallest of atoms.

Finally, Brahma says to Goddess Durga that after he sent Kama, Rati and Spring to enchant Shiva, Shiva did not even look at them. Shiva is detached from the world, is a yogi and doesn't desire a wife.

Brahma asks Durga to make Shiva want a wife, because only she can captivate Shiva. He asks her to be born as Daksha's daughter and become Shiva's wife. He explains that since Shiva rebuked him for his desires, Shiva would never ask for a wife, unless Durga influences him.

Brahma tells Durga that, because he wants creation to move forward, he asks for her help. He says that neither Vishnu nor Lakshmi nor Kama are capable of charming Shiva, only she can do it. He then mentions that Daksha is already performing penance to seek her blessings to be born as his daughter.

Durga, surprised by Brahma's words, realizes that a delusion has affected Brahma that makes him want to charm Shiva. She realizes that Brahma wants power from her to charm Shiva. She then thinks about how she can't disobey Brahma, as that would cause problems with the Vedas. She knows that Shiva is the Parabrahman and not a mere deva or Brahma's son, so it's wrong to attempt to charm him, but she also realizes if Shiva doesn't marry, creation would stop.

She then realizes she has to give Brahma what he wants. She tells Brahma that there is no other women who can charm Shiva. She says that, if Shiva does not get a wife, then the creation won't continue. She will take birth as Sati and be Shiva's wife, and she will make Shiva subservient to her, through her devotion, just like ordinary mortals are to their wives.

After saying this, Durga disappears. Brahma, happy and hopeful, goes to his sons to narrate all that has happened.

Chapter Twelve

(DAKSHA RECEIVES THE BOON)

Narada asks Brahma to explain how Daksha secured his boon from the Goddess and how she became his daughter. Brahma tells him how Daksha, followed his advice and began his penance.

Daksha went to the northern shore of the milky ocean, and for three thousand divine years, he practiced intense penance. He controlled his mind, sustained himself on air, water and leaves, and continuously meditated upon the Goddess.

Finally, Goddess Durga appeared before Daksha, in her cosmic form. Daksha, feeling blessed, praised her and bowed down before her, offering his prayers. He calls her the mother of the universe and praises her form.

The Goddess, pleased with Daksha's devotion, asks him to choose a boon. Daksha asks her, if she wants to give him a boon, then he asks that she take birth as his daughter. He tells her that Rudra has manifested himself, but is alone and detached and so, only she will be able to charm him. He wants her to be born as his daughter and be Shiva's wife.

Goddess Durga smiles and agrees to be born as Daksha's daughter, and be Shiva's wife. She tells Daksha that, she is pleased with his devotion and, she will take birth as his daughter, but she will have to first perform penance for it, and secure a boon from Shiva. She explains that she is Shiva's eternal consort and, because of his grace, she will take birth as his wife.

Before granting the boon, the Goddess tells Daksha that he must make a promise. She says that, if he ever disrespects her in the future, she will immediately leave her body and return to her original form or take up another form. Daksha accepts this promise. Durga then tells him, that at every creation, she will take birth as his daughter and become Shiva's beloved.

After this, Goddess Durga vanished. Daksha, overjoyed, returned to his hermitage, knowing that the Goddess would be born as his daughter.

Chapter Thirteen

(NARADA'S CURSES AND DAKSHA'S LOSS)

This chapter of the Shiva Purana tells the story of how Daksha, a powerful being, tried to populate the world with his sons but was thwarted by Narada, a celestial sage, not once, but twice. It all starts after Daksha happily returns home after the previous events. He attempts to create offspring through mind, which is unsuccessful, prompting him to ask Brahma (his father).

Brahma advises Daksha to marry Asikni, the daughter of Pancajana, and create through physical union. Daksha follows this advice and has thousands of sons called the Haryashvas, who are diligent and follow the Vedic ways. Daksha, wanting to ensure a large population, orders his sons to create offspring. The Haryashvas go to a holy lake, where their minds become clear.

Narada, knowing that this creation is not what Lord Shiva desires, appears before the Haryashvas and questions their knowledge of the world before beginning to create life. Intrigued by Narada's words and contemplating what he said, the Haryashvas, without hesitation or any resistance, abandon their plan. They decide to follow a path of no return.

Daksha, devastated when he finds out his sons did not return, is consoled by Brahma, who tells him fate is powerful. Daksha then has another set of a thousand sons, the Sabalashvas. Daksha's new sons follow the footsteps of their elder brothers and go to the same place and follow the same process.

Narada again appears and speaks to the Sabalashvas, who then follow the same path of no return as their elder brothers.

Daksha is hit by another great loss when he realizes that his second set of sons also failed to return. It is then he finds out that Narada is behind it all. Daksha, consumed with grief and anger, calls Narada a wicked, ruthless rogue and curses Narada, saying he would never be steady and roam the world forever.

Narada, completely unaffected, accepts the curse. The text explains that Daksha's anger and lack of understanding was due to Lord Shiva's illusion. It also states that saintly Brahmins accept curses with forbearance.

Chapter Fourteen

(THE BIRTH OF SATI AND HER CHILDHOOD)

This chapter tells the story of the birth of Sati (also known as Uma), an incarnation of the Divine Mother, as Daksha's daughter. It begins with Brahma, the creator, visiting Daksha to console him after the events of the previous chapter, making peace between Daksha and Narada. Brahma also arranges marriages for Daksha's sixty daughters, ten to Dharma, thirteen to Sage Kashyapa, twenty-seven to the Moon, and two each to Bhrigu, Angiras, and Krsasva, and the remaining to Tarksya. The offspring of these unions go on to populate the world. Then, Daksha and his wife think of the Divine Mother, wanting a daughter who is divine.

The Divine Mother, pleased by their devotion, decides to incarnate as their daughter. Through a mental message, she lets Daksha know of her intent. An auspicious hour arrives, and Daksha's wife, Virini, conceives. All the signs of pregnancy are visible and Virini shines with an aura of peace. Daksha, filled with joy, performs rituals and gives gifts. Vishnu and other gods visit Virini, praising her and the future divine child.

After nine months, on a favorable astrological day, the Divine Mother appears as a baby, a luminous figure. Daksha knows immediately that she is the Divine Goddess herself. A soft rain falls, flowers blossom, the directions become calm, and musical instruments are played by the Gods. Daksha is overjoyed.

Daksha praises the Divine Mother, acknowledging her role in creation, preservation, and destruction. He knows that those who meditate on her attain both worldly happiness and liberation. He calls her Bhavani, Ambika, Jaganmaya, and Durga.

The Goddess then speaks to Daksha, making sure only he can hear her. She tells him that she will be born as his daughter to fulfill his wishes, and urges him to continue with his penance. Then, she takes on the form of an infant. The cries of the baby bring joy to everyone. Daksha and Virini, delighted with their daughter's beauty, perform all the traditional ceremonies, offering gifts to Brahmins.

Gods and Sages arrive to celebrate, praising the Divine Mother and congratulating Daksha and Virini. Daksha, upon their advice, names her Uma. They say that she will have other names in the future that are auspicious and will remove suffering. They all then returned to their respective abodes, remembering Siva along with Uma.

Uma is cared for and grows like the moon, gaining new qualities each day. As a child, Uma draws pictures of Shiva and sings songs in his name, remembering him as Sthanu, Rudra, and the destroyer of Kama, showing her devotion to him from a young age. Daksha and Virini find her devotion is increasing day by day even as a child. She brings joy and happiness to her home.

Chapter Fifteen

(SATI'S PENANCE AND THE DEVAS' HYMN TO SHIVA)

This chapter describes Sati's intense devotion to Lord Shiva and the subsequent praise offered by the Devas. It begins with Brahma recounting a time he and Narada saw Sati at Daksha's home. She respectfully bows to them and Brahma blesses her saying that she will have Lord Shiva as her husband. Brahma emphasizes that Shiva is unlike anyone else, a unique being who will desire only her. Daksha is delighted to hear this.

Sati grows into a beautiful young woman, and she too desires to have Shiva as her husband. With her mother's permission, she starts a series of sacred rites to propitiate Shiva, spending several months in specific worship. Each month, she worships Shiva with various offerings such as rice with jaggery and salt, pies and puddings, barley with gingelly seeds, and keeps fasts. She does these worship with great devotion and commitment. She performs these acts of devotion at various times of the lunar cycle and also keeps herself awake whole night.

Finally, Sati ends all sacred rites, and with total focus, meditates on Shiva, not thinking of anyone else. The Devas and Sages, led by Vishnu and Brahma, are astonished by her intense penance. They admire her devotion, realizing she embodies success and enlightenment. They respectfully bow to her with joy.

The Devas and Sages then proceed to Kailasa, the abode of Shiva. There, they, along with Vishnu, Lakshmi, Brahma, and Savitri, praise Shiva with beautiful hymns.

In their hymns, the Devas acknowledge Shiva as the source of all creation, the supreme being, the soul of the universe, and the ultimate goal of all devotees. They call him Mahesha, Purusha, and Atman, acknowledging him as the one who creates, sustains, controls, and ultimately dissolves everything. They recognize that Shiva transcends everything, is beyond definition, and manifests in various forms through Maya.

They express that Shiva is the light of knowledge, the bestower of salvation, and the one who can liberate beings from the cycle of birth and death. They praise him as the one who is beyond the reach of fools but lives in the hearts of the wise. They acknowledge his infinite power, his formless and immense forms, and his role in the creation and dissolution of the universe. They declare him as their protector and refuge and as the embodiment of all that is. The Devas express their devotion to Shiva and his devotees.

The Devas recognize that the whole world, with all the beings, is a creation of Shiva with the difference of name and form. They understand that the world goes through phases of creation and destruction similar to the flames of fire and the sun. They conclude that Shiva is beyond all labels, being neither Deva nor Asura, neither man nor woman, neither existent nor non-existent, but something that is beyond all these definitions. They praise him as the Lord of Yoga whom Yogis are able to realize.

After offering their elaborate hymn, the Devas, including Vishnu and the other gods, stand silently in front of Lord Shiva, their shoulders bent in deep devotion.

Chapter Sixteen

(BRAHMA AND VISHNU'S PRAYER TO SHIVA)

This chapter starts with Shiva being happy after listening to prayers by Vishnu and others. He smiles and asks Brahma and Vishnu, along with other gods and sages, why they've come. Brahma explains that they have all come to ask something important of Shiva. They say the world needs Shiva's help to defeat demons.

Brahma points out that while he creates, Vishnu protects, and Shiva destroys, they are all still part of one whole. He explains that Shiva is like the heart from which the others came. He further says that they need Shiva to take a wife. It's essential for the world's well-being as they cannot perform their duties alone. Brahma reminds Shiva of his own words, how he would be called Rudra, and would marry to perform these duties. He also emphasizes that they are unable to handle the creation, maintenance and destruction without Shiva.

Shiva replies that he is happy to see them and they are very dear to him but, he is detached, focused on penance and is not interested in marriage. He says marriage is a big bondage for someone like him. However, he also says he's willing to help them, as he always is for his devotees, and for the greater good. Shiva says that his wife should be a yogini (one who practices yoga) during his penance and a loving wife when he desires love. She should also not disturb him when he meditates. If she ever doubts him, he says he would leave her.

Brahma agrees and suggests Uma. He says she was once Saraswati (his wife) and Lakshmi (Vishnu's wife), and from her desire for the welfare of the world she has taken a third form as Daksha's daughter, Sati. She is already practicing penance to marry Shiva. She will be an ideal partner to

Shiva as she is dedicated, powerful and desires him deeply as her husband. Brahma asks Shiva to marry her out of mercy.

Vishnu also agrees with Brahma and asks Shiva to accept Sati to bring happiness in the world. He assures Shiva that he agrees to all which Brahma has said.

Lastly, Shiva says "So be it" to their requests. Brahma and Vishnu then happily return home, taking the gods, goddesses, and sages with them.

Chapter Seventeen

(SATI RECEIVES A BLESSING AND SHIVA'S REQUEST)

Brahma continues the story, explaining that after the gods' request, Sati, Daksha's daughter, starts observing a special fast. She worships Shiva with great devotion. While she meditates, Shiva appears before her in a beautiful form - he is fair, handsome, with five faces, three eyes, a crescent moon on his forehead, and a blue neck. He holds a trident and an amulet and is radiating a powerful light. He's a vision of beauty.

Sati, shy at first, bows down at his feet. Shiva, knowing her desire to marry him, still wants her to ask for a boon (a special wish). He asks her what she desires. Sati, very shy, is unable to speak at first. Shiva asks her again and again. Finally, suppressing her shyness, Sati asks for Shiva as her husband. Shiva immediately grants her the boon and says, "You be my wife."

Sati is overjoyed and doesn't say anything, her heart filled with happiness. She expresses her love through subtle gestures, and a deep romantic connection grows between them.

Sati then asks Shiva to marry her with proper rituals in front of her father. Shiva, pleased with her devotion, says "So be it". Sati bows down to Shiva and returns home to her mother, full of happiness.

Meanwhile, Shiva goes back to his hermitage in the Himalayas but, he feels the pangs of separation from Sati. Although he usually remains detached in meditation, he now longs for her. He remembers Brahma and, through his meditative powers, summons him.

Brahma and Saraswati arrive at Shiva's place in the Himalayas. Shiva, embarrassed for his feelings, says he's being a little selfish by wanting a wife. He tells Brahma how Sati had asked to marry him in front of her father. Shiva admits that he agreed, being pleased with her devotion. Shiva then asks Brahma to go to Daksha and ask for Sati's hand in marriage. Shiva is impatient and wants the separation to end quickly. He wants Brahma to find all ways to cut short her days of separation from her.

Brahma is happy to help and assures Shiva that Daksha will agree to the marriage. Brahma then flies to Daksha's home.

Meanwhile, Sati reaches her home and pays respect to her parents. Her friends and relatives tell her parents about the boon she had received from Shiva. The parents celebrate the event with a big feast, giving gifts to Brahmins and those in need. They were very happy for their daughter. Daksha starts to worry about how to give his daughter to Shiva.

While Daksha was wondering how to do all of this, Brahma arrives with Saraswati. Daksha welcomes them with great respect. He asks the purpose of their visit.

Brahma tells Daksha that he has come to talk about Sati and Shiva's marriage. He tells him that Sati has already received a boon to marry Shiva, so the time is now right for them to marry. Brahma explains that Shiva is also separated from Sati and has become restless with feelings, giving up his meditation. He explains how he (Shiva) constantly repeats the question about Sati's whereabouts. He says Shiva is longing for Sati as much as she is for him.

Brahma tells Daksha that Sati has won over Shiva. He asks Daksha to give Sati to Shiva, promising that Shiva and Sati's marriage would make everyone happy. He also says that he will bring Shiva to Daksha's home to wed Sati. Daksha is overjoyed and immediately agrees to the marriage. He feels relieved and agrees.

Brahma, satisfied with Daksha's acceptance, returns happily to where Shiva was. Meanwhile, Daksha, with his wife and daughter, are also delighted, feeling like they have been filled with nectar.

Chapter Eighteen

(THE STORY OF SHIVA AND SATI'S WEDDING)

The chapter begins with Narada asking Brahma about what happened when Brahma went to see Lord Shiva. Brahma tells Narada that he was very happy to go to the Himalayas to bring Shiva back to Daksha's house. When Shiva saw Brahma coming, he wondered if it was about marrying Sati. Shiva, even though he's a great god, acted like a normal person because he loves Sati so much.

Shiva asked Brahma about Sati, worried that he might be separated from her. He said that the worry of being apart was hurting him and not Sati. He also said, that Sati is no different from him and he should get Sati. Then, Shiva asked Brahma to help him achieve this marriage.

Brahma, after hearing how much Shiva wanted to marry Sati, said that Daksha, Sati's father, had already agreed. Daksha told Brahma that Sati was meant for Shiva and he would give her to Shiva. Daksha requested Shiva to come to his house during an auspicious time so that he could offer his daughter to Shiva as a gift.

When Shiva heard this news from Brahma, he was happy and agreed to go to Daksha's house with Brahma and Narada. Shiva also asked Brahma to remember all of Brahma's mental and physical sons, like Marici, and that they would all go together with Shiva's attendants.

Following Shiva's request, Brahma then called all his sons and Narada, who all came happily. Vishnu, another great god and a big fan of Shiva, also arrived with his wife Lakshmi, riding his eagle Garuda, and his army. On a Sunday, the thirteenth day of the bright part of the month of Chaitra, during a lucky time, Shiva started his journey to Daksha's house. Everyone, including Brahma, Vishnu, and many sages, went with him, creating a very bright and happy procession.

Along the way, Shiva and his followers celebrated with lots of fun, music, and dance. They made ornaments of all the strange things that Shiva has, like elephant skin, snakes, and the moon in his hair look beautiful. Soon, Shiva reached Daksha's home quickly on his bull, along with everyone else. Daksha greeted everyone with much respect and joy.

Daksha honoured the gods, sages, and Shiva's followers. He then took Shiva inside his house, offered him a seat and worshipped him with a lot of devotion. Daksha also worshipped Vishnu, Brahma, other wise men, gods, and Shiva's Ganas (group of attendants). After the worship, Daksha announced in front of everyone that the marriage would take place. Daksha also requested Brahma to perform the marriage rites and Brahma agreed with pleasure.

On an auspicious day and time, Daksha gave his daughter, Sati, to Shiva. As part of the marriage tradition, Shiva happily held Sati's hand. Everyone, including Vishnu, Brahma, and all the other sages, praised Shiva with hymns and bowed to him. There was a grand celebration with singing and dancing. Daksha was very happy after giving his daughter away, and Sati and Shiva were also in a happy mood. The whole event concluded auspiciously.

Chapter Nineteen

(THE STORY OF THE WEDDING AND A STRANGE INCIDENT)

After Daksha gave his daughter Sati in marriage to Shiva, he gave a lot of gifts, like dowry and money, to Shiva and all the Brahmins. Then, Vishnu, along with his wife Lakshmi, came to Shiva. Vishnu said that Shiva and Sati are like the parents of the world, who take birth to help good people and punish the bad ones. He also pointed out how Shiva and Sati are fair and dark-skinned, like how Vishnu and Lakshmi are dark and fair-skinned, and he asked Shiva and Sati to always protect good people and bring happiness to the world. Vishnu also requested Shiva that anyone who looks at Sati with bad intentions should be killed.

Shiva agreed to Vishnu's requests and laughed. After that, Vishnu went back home, keeping the request a secret. Then, Brahma, started all the wedding rituals. Shiva and Sati walked around the sacred fire as part of the wedding ceremony. Afterwards, everyone celebrated with music, dance, and lots of fun.

During the ceremony, a very surprising thing happened. Brahma said that Shiva's magic (Maya) is very tricky and can fool anyone and everyone. Brahma admitted that he had tried to trick Shiva before, but now Shiva's magic was working on him. Brahma also said that if you wish bad things for others, you end up getting the same bad things for yourself. He also mentioned that people should not wish bad things to others.

While walking around the fire, Sati's feet became visible. Brahma got distracted and started looking at her. He couldn't stop looking at her and got feelings of love. Then, he really wanted to see her face but Sati was hiding her face because she was shy. Then, Brahma created a smoky fire so that everyone couldn't see properly. When Shiva covered his eyes because of the smoke, Brahma quickly lifted Sati's veil and looked at her face multiple times. As a result, his semen fell on the ground, which is considered a very big sin.

Shiva saw this with his divine eyes and got very angry. He told Brahma that he had done a terrible thing by looking at Sati with lust during her wedding. Shiva said that he knows everything in the world, and nothing is hidden from him. Shiva got so angry that he was ready to kill Brahma.

When Shiva was about to kill Brahma with his trident, everyone was very scared. The gods and sages started praying to Shiva, asking him to forgive Brahma. They said that Shiva is the father of the universe, and Sati is the mother, and everyone else, including Vishnu and Brahma, are his helpers. They also said that Shiva's magic is very confusing, and everyone gets tricked by it.

Daksha rushed towards Shiva, asking him to not harm Brahma. Shiva remembered Vishnu's earlier request that anyone who looks at Sati with lust should be killed, and said that he would fulfill his promise by killing Brahma. Shiva says that Brahma has looked at Sati lustfully and has committed the sin of discharging his semen, which is why Shiva should kill him.

Vishnu, who is very smart and a big fan of Shiva, stepped in. He praised Shiva and begged him not to kill Brahma, saying that Brahma is the creator of the world and if he's killed, no one will be there to create. Vishnu also reminded Shiva that all three of them: Shiva, Vishnu and Brahma, are carrying out the functions of creation, sustenance and dissolution as instructed by Siva. Vishnu pleaded that Brahma himself helped to get Sati married to Shiva.

Shiva refused Vishnu's plea. He said that even though Vishnu is very dear to him, he won't stop himself from killing Brahma. He will create all the living beings himself or by creating another creator and says that he is firm on his decision of killing Brahma.

Vishnu smiled and asked Shiva not to kill himself, because all three of them (Shiva, Vishnu, and Brahma) are the same, with the same body. Vishnu explained that they all are part of Shiva's power; and that each of them perform different functions for the good of the world. He mentioned that the three of them are like parts of the same body, with their own specific purposes. Vishnu also explained that Shiva is the supreme being, and that he is present everywhere in the universe. He described Shiva as the ultimate truth, formless and eternal, from whom everything comes from.

Hearing this, Shiva was very happy and did not kill Brahma. The chapter ends with everyone feeling relieved and happy because Shiva's anger was calmed and a great disaster was averted.

Chapter Twenty

(THE STORY AFTER THE WEDDING TROUBLE)

The chapter starts with Narada asking Brahma what happened after Shiva stopped being angry with Brahma. Brahma explains that when Shiva decided not to kill him, everyone became happy and fearless. All the gods, sages, and people bowed to Shiva and praised him with love.

Shiva was happy and spoke to Brahma in front of everyone. Shiva told Brahma he was glad and asked him to not be afraid. Shiva also asked Brahma to touch his head with his hand and follow his orders. When Brahma did that, he changed into the shape of a bull, which is Shiva's ride. Brahma was ashamed to be seen like that by everyone including Indra and other devas.

Brahma felt very embarrassed, bowed to Shiva again and again, and asked for forgiveness. He also wanted to know how to get rid of his sin and said that even death is a small punishment for his sin.

Shiva told Brahma that he would have to do penance, happily, in the form of a bull, to please Shiva. Shiva said that Brahma would become famous as "The head of Rudra" and help Brahmins with their rituals. He also said that because Brahma had acted like a normal human by discharging semen, he would be born as a human and roam the earth. When he would roam the earth in the form of a bull, people will ask, "What is there on the head of Brahma?" and he would have to say "Shiva". Shiva also mentioned that any person who has committed a similar sin (outraging modesty of another's wife) will be freed from that sin by listening to this story. He will get rid of sin every time people talk about this wrong thing that Brahma did, becoming pure eventually. Shiva says that he will have to tolerate people ridiculing him and this is the penance for his sin. Shiva also told him that the semen drops that fell on the ground will become dangerous clouds.

Right then, four dangerous clouds appeared from the semen drops. These clouds were called Samvartaka, Avarta, Puskara, and Drona. They roared and showered with deadly powers, but Shiva and Sati were calm.

After that, Brahma finished the remaining wedding rituals. The gods showered flowers on Shiva and Sati. The wives of the gods celebrated with music and songs. The celestial dancers, like Rambha, danced with joy.

Shiva, pleased with how well the wedding was performed, asked Brahma what gift he wanted as payment for being the priest. Shiva said he could grant him anything. Brahma requested that in order to purify people from sins, Shiva and Sati should stay at that place in that very form. Brahma also said that he would stay nearby and do penance to get rid of his sin.

Brahma also requested that anyone who visits that place on the thirteenth day of the bright half of Chaitra (March-April), when the star is Uttaraphalguni, and the day is Sunday, should have their sins removed. He also mentioned that women with problems like being barren, ugly, or unlucky, would be free from those problems if they visited that place. Shiva was happy and said, "Let it be so." He then created a partial image of himself and Sati and stayed at the altar as Brahma requested.

Shiva, with his wife Sati, prepared to leave. Daksha, Vishnu, all the gods, and Shiva's followers praised Shiva with joy. Shiva then made Sati sit on the bull and they both went to the Himalayas. Everyone was very happy and excited, but also a bit sad to see Shiva leave.

Some played instruments, others sang praises of Shiva, and they all followed him happily. Halfway, Shiva bid farewell to Daksha who returned to his home. Vishnu and other gods kept following Shiva even after being told to go back, because of their love for Shiva. Shiva, his wife Sati, and his followers went to the beautiful Himalayas where they were very happy. Shiva then honored and said goodbye to the gods and sages who went back home with happy faces. Shiva and Sati then played together in the Himalayas. Eventually, Shiva, Sati and all his followers went to their residence in Kailasa.

Brahma ends by saying that he told Narada how Shiva and Sati got married. He says that if anyone listens to this story with devotion during marriages or other good events, the ceremonies will always go well. Also, the bride will be blessed with happiness and good character and will have children by listening to this story.

Chapter Twenty One

(SHIVA AND SATI'S PLAYFUL TIME)

The chapter begins with Narada praising Brahma for his wonderful storytelling about Shiva and Sati's marriage. Narada, who is always eager to know more, asks Brahma to continue sharing the stories of the divine couple.

Brahma agrees and says that he will tell how Shiva spent his time with Sati after their marriage. After reaching their beautiful home in the Himalayas, Shiva and Sati got off the bull. Shiva, along with Sati, went into their room, where they were very happy. Shiva, acting like people in the world do, then asked his attendants, like Nandin, to leave. Shiva told them to only come back when he remembers them.

Once Shiva was alone with Sati, they were full of joy. He played with her in many ways. Sometimes, he would pick flowers and make a garland for her neck. When Sati looked at her reflection in a mirror, Shiva would peep into it to see his own face next to hers. Shiva would play with her earrings, touching them and cleaning them himself. He would color her feet red with a special dye. He whispered sweet things into her ears, just to see her face when she turned to look at him.

Shiva would often go away and suddenly come back to close her eyes from behind. He would then ask her to guess his name. Sometimes, he would become invisible using his powers and then embrace her when she was not expecting it. He would put musk on her breasts, drawing marks like bees. He would take off her necklaces and press her breasts gently with his hands. He would remove her bracelets and bangles and then put them back on. Sometimes, he would look at the dark spot on her breasts and jokingly compare it to her name "Kalika".

Shiva and Sati talked sweetly to each other and laughed a lot. Shiva picked lotuses and other beautiful flowers to decorate her and make her more beautiful. They would roam around the mountains together. Shiva did not want to do anything without her. He was not happy, even for a moment, if she was not with him.

After spending much time together, Shiva remembered Kama and spring arrived because of him. The trees were filled with flowers, the water was covered with lotuses, and bees were buzzing everywhere. The gentle wind was full of the smell of sweet flowers. The flowers looked like the arrows of Kama, the god of love. The lakes were shining and the wind was like a lovely woman trying to attract everyone with her beautiful face. Mango trees were shining like beds for Kama's arrows. The lakes looked like pure minds, reflecting the supreme truth. The dew drops shone brightly like the hearts of good people. The nights were clear and beautiful. It was a perfect setting for love.

Shiva and Sati spent a lot of time enjoying the mountains and rivers. They were together all the time. Sati was so special that Shiva could not have any peace without her. She gave him total happiness. Sati filled his mind and he seemed to be a part of her. Shiva enjoyed making garlands for Sati and felt great joy in her presence. They would talk, laugh, and look at each other with love. He was captivated by her beauty and her playful jokes, like a huge elephant that can't move when tied by ropes. Shiva stayed with Sati in the mountains for many years, enjoying their time together. According to the calculations of the devas, this lasted for twenty five years.

Chapter Twenty Two

(SATI'S CONCERNS AND SHIVA'S REASSURANCES)

The chapter starts with Sati speaking to Shiva while they are on the Kailasa mountain. Sati tells Shiva that the rainy season has begun. She describes how dark clouds have filled the sky, with thunder and lightning. She says the wind is blowing water everywhere and the trees are moving a lot. She mentions that the sun and the moon are hidden by the clouds, making the day feel like night, and people who are away from their lovers are sad. Sati says that the heavy rains and winds are scary. She notes how trees are being broken, and that even birds like cranes are flying in the sky. She also mentions how the lightning is like a fire. Sati points out that even plants are growing everywhere, even in temples. She feels that the rainy season is troublesome and she doesn't like it.

Sati tells Shiva that even peacocks and deer are in distress. She points out how some birds are building nests, but they don't have a home yet and without a home how will they be happy. Sati says that she is scared of the rain and asks Shiva to build them a home. She suggests they could live on Kailasa, the Himalayas, or in Mahakasi.

Shiva laughs at Sati's concerns, making the moon on his head shine brighter with its light. Shiva tells Sati that the clouds won't reach the place where he will make their home. He explains that clouds only stay around the lower parts of the Himalayas and never go to the top. He also says that clouds don't go above Mount Sumeru. Shiva asks Sati to choose where she would like to live and assures her she would be very happy in that place.

Shiva describes the Himalayas as a place where bees sing sweet songs. He says that the women of Siddha will welcome her, and the daughters of snakes and other celestial ladies will also greet her with happiness. Shiva mentions that even Menaka, the wife of the king of the mountains, will be very nice to her. He also mentions that the ladies of the Himalaya's family will share great wisdom with her and will help her in any way possible.

Shiva says that the Himalayas are always like spring, filled with flowers, trees, cool lakes, and cuckoos. It's full of grass, and many animals and birds. The mountains are full of precious stones and the lakes are filled with lotus flowers, with crocodiles and other sea creatures. He mentions various types of beautiful trees and birds that live there. The lakes are full of fragrant saffron and blue lotuses. Even the trees seem to be dancing. He also speaks about Mount Meru, where the gods live and which is a beautiful and magical place.

Shiva asks Sati if she wants to stay in the beautiful Himalayas, or in his own Kailasa, or Mount Meru. He tells her that he will prepare whichever place she chooses for their home.

Sati tells Shiva that she wants to live on the Himalayas. Shiva, is delighted at her choice, and immediately takes her to the top of the mountain.

They arrive at a beautiful mountaintop, where the Siddha women live. It's a place with colorful gems, lotuses, lakes, and forests. Shiva and Sati spend a lot of time there, enjoying the beautiful surroundings. The place is full of trees, flowers, lakes, and lots of birds. There are various kinds of semi-divine

beings living there. The celestial women dance and sing, making the place very happy and lively.

Shiva and Sati spend ten thousand years together in this beautiful place, enjoying each other's company. They visit different places, like Mount Meru, different continents, and forests. Shiva enjoys his time with Sati more than anything else. They are always looking at each other, which only increases their love. They nurture their love every day by seeing each other, talking to each other and just being with each other. They love being together more than anything else.

Chapter Twenty Three

(SATI'S QUESTION ABOUT DEVOTION)

The chapter begins with Brahma explaining that after enjoying many years with Shiva, Sati began to feel less attached to worldly pleasures. She had been happy and playful with Shiva for long but now she was having different thoughts.

One day, after showing her love and respect to Shiva, Sati asks him a question. She calls him the greatest lord, full of mercy and compassion, and asks him to have pity on her. Sati says that Shiva is beyond all qualities and is both with and without form. She says that she was blessed to be his wife. She also tells him that she feels satisfied with the worldly pleasures of their love and now she wants to know how people can overcome suffering quickly. Sati requests Shiva to share what action can help people achieve the highest state and break free from the bondage of the world.

Shiva, understanding that Sati is asking for the benefit of all beings, tells her that he will explain the secret to liberation. He says that true knowledge, the understanding that "I am Brahman," is very rare. He explains that devotion to him is the key to both worldly pleasures and salvation and that this can be achieved by his grace. He also says that devotion and true knowledge are not different and that a person devoted to him experiences unending happiness. Shiva also mentions that because of his love for devotion, he goes to the homes of even the poorest people.

Different Types of Devotion

Shiva describes different kinds of devotion like with form and without form, natural and forced, great and small, and lasting and temporary. He also talks about the 9 main ways to be devoted.

The Nine Aspects of Devotion

Shiva explains the nine ways to show devotion:

1. **Listening:** To hear stories about Shiva with love.

2. **Eulogizing:** To praise Shiva's qualities out loud.

3. **Remembering:** To always keep Shiva in your mind.

4. **Serving:** To serve Shiva with your body, mind, and speech.

5. **Surrendering:** To give yourself completely to Shiva with a feeling of happiness.

6. **Worshipping:** To offer sixteen types of service to Shiva.

7. **Saluting:** To meditate on Shiva, chant mantras and bow to him touching the ground with 8 limbs.

8. **Friendliness:** To believe that whatever Shiva gives, is always for your good.

9. **Dedication:** To give everything to Shiva without keeping anything for yourself.

Shiva says that these nine aspects of devotion lead to true knowledge, worldly pleasures, and salvation and make him happy. He says that devotion is as dear to him as Sati is. He mentions that devotion is the easiest and most pleasing path in the world and is particularly powerful in the Kali Yuga. He also explains that in this age, knowledge and detachment have become difficult to achieve.

Shiva says that he is controlled by devotion and always helps his devotees and removes all obstacles from their path and punishes those who do not have devotion. He recalls how he saved his devotees, burned the God of Death, punished the sun, and rejected Ravana, just for the sake of his devotees. He says that he is always there for those who are devoted to him.

Brahma says that when Sati heard about the power of devotion, she was delighted and bowed to Shiva. She then asked him more questions about virtue, righteousness, and other sacred teachings that would benefit all creatures.

Shiva was happy with her questions and explained everything in detail about morality, sacred chants, the duties of kings, sons, and wives, knowledge about medicine, astrology, palmistry etc.

Brahma says that Shiva and Sati, who are the Supreme Brahman, and the givers of happiness to the world, lived and played in many places, always helping people.

Chapter Twenty Four

(THE STORY OF SATI, SHIVA, AND RAMA)

The chapter starts with Narada asking Brahma to tell him more about the wonderful stories of Shiva and Sati. He wants to know what the couple did after they stayed on the mountain.

Brahma explains that after enjoying their time together, Shiva and Sati followed worldly traditions. He says that, as part of their story, Sati and Shiva were separated for a while. Brahma also clarifies that Shiva and Shakti (Sati) are always united, like a word and its meaning, and their separation is just part of their divine play. He mentions that Sati was later abandoned by Shiva at her father's sacrifice. Because of disrespect to Shiva she gave up her body. She was born again as Parvati and married Shiva again.

Narada is confused. He asks Brahma why Shiva abandoned his wife, who was very dear to him. He also wants to know why Daksha disrespected Shiva, how Sati died, and what happened after that.

Brahma tells Narada that everything is part of Shiva's divine play. Shiva is the supreme being that everyone worships. He is beyond blame and is the cause of everything.

Brahma continues the story and says that one day, Shiva and Sati were travelling on Earth. They reach Dandaka forest where Shiva sees Rama searching for Sita, who was kidnapped by Ravana. Rama was in great distress and crying for Sita. He was walking around the forest with his brother Lakshmana, looking very sad. Shiva, who is very kind to his devotees, happily bowed to Rama. Sati was confused to see Shiva bowing to a human being.

Sati asks Shiva who these two sad people are. She questions why Shiva is behaving like a devotee to the one who looks like a blue lotus (referring to Rama's dark skin). She thinks it's strange that a master is bowing to a servant.

Shiva laughs and tells Sati that the two men are Rama and Lakshmana, the sons of Dasaratha. He explains that Lakshmana is a partial incarnation of Sesa and that the older one, Rama is a full incarnation of Vishnu. Shiva also mentioned that Rama had come to earth to protect the good.

Even after hearing Shiva, Sati's mind is not convinced. Shiva, knowing this, tells Sati that she can test Rama to find out if he is truly divine. He asks her to go near him and see for herself.

Sati goes to where Rama was standing under a Banyan tree. She decides to test Rama by taking the form of Sita and going to him. She thinks if Rama is Vishnu he will recognize the truth.

When Sati, disguised as Sita, goes to Rama, Rama calls her 'Sati', realizes who she is and laughs. He asks her where Shiva is, and why she is alone. He also asks why she has taken the form of Sita.

Sati is stunned by Rama's knowledge. She remembers what Shiva had said, and understands that Rama is truly Vishnu. She feels ashamed for doubting Shiva's words. She returns to her real form and remembers Shiva.

Sati tells Rama that Shiva had come there and bowed to him with respect. She explains how Shiva's words had made her doubt his divinity, which is why she had wanted to test him. Sati says that she realized that Rama was truly Vishnu, but she is still confused how he is worthy of being worshipped by Shiva.

Rama smiles when he heard Sati's words and remembers Shiva in his heart. He is filled with love for Shiva. Without the explicit permission of Sati, he does not go near Shiva, but praises the greatness of Shiva to Sati.

Chapter Twenty Five

(THE STORY OF VISHNU'S CORONATION AND SATI'S SEPARATION)

The chapter begins with Rama telling Sati a story about how Shiva had once called the divine architect, Vishwakarma, to build a beautiful hall and throne in his cowshed. He invited all the gods and goddesses, as well as Brahma and the sages, to a great ceremony. He had musicians play instruments and had sixteen virgins from different groups present for the occasion. Shiva filled five pots with holy water from different rivers.

Rama then tells Sati how, Shiva called Vishnu and made him sit on a beautiful throne in a specific auspicious time. Shiva then crowned Vishnu, tied a holy thread around his waist and gave him many boons. Vishnu was made worthy of respect of all gods and the Vedas at Shiva's bidding.

Shiva himself bowed to Vishnu, showing his respect. He told everyone that Vishnu would be the creator, sustainer, and destroyer of the worlds. He also said that Vishnu would be the bestower of virtues and the punisher of evil and that Vishnu will also be invincible in battle, even against Shiva. He gave Vishnu the power of will and said that Vishnu would be able to perform many divine plays. Shiva also said that he would punish anyone who hated Vishnu and give salvation to Vishnu's followers. He also gives him Maya power that can delude everyone in the world.

Shiva called Vishnu his left hand and Brahma his right hand. He said that Rudra is his heart and is worthy of the respect of everyone. Shiva also said that Vishnu would take different forms on Earth to protect it, and that his place would be known as Goloka, a place of great brilliance. Shiva then said that he would witness Vishnu's incarnations on earth and be happy.

After giving Vishnu all these blessings, Shiva returned to Kailasa with Sati. Vishnu then took the form of a cowherd, wandering around with his followers. Vishnu then took a fourfold incarnation as Rama and his brothers (Bharat, Lakshmana, and Shatrughna). Rama explains that he was in the forest at the request of his father but unfortunately, his wife Sita has been kidnapped by a demon. He tells Sati that he was looking for Sita and was separated from his family. Rama says he is happy to see Sati and is confident that he will find his wife because of her blessings.

Rama, after praising Sati, asks for her leave and then he leaves. Sati is happy with Rama's words and his devotion to Shiva. Sati feels guilty for doubting Rama and she thinks she should have listened to Shiva in the first place. She feels sad for doubting Rama and starts to worry about what she will say to Shiva.

When Sati returns to Shiva, she is pale and worried. Shiva knows what has happened and asks her if she is done testing Rama. Sati does not say anything, but looks down, ashamed. Shiva realizes that he has to abide by the promise he had made when he was angry with Vishnu. Shiva had promised that anyone who looks at Sati with bad intentions should be punished. Even though it was his own wife, he cannot go back on his promise.

Shiva decides that he will have to mentally leave Sati and leave. Shiva understands that if he keeps loving Sati as before, he will break his promise. So, without telling her why, he mentally gives up Sati. He returns home, but does not reveal his promise.

While they are traveling, a heavenly voice speaks out loud that no one is as great as Shiva and he has fulfilled his promise. Hearing this, Sati asks Shiva what the promise is but Shiva does not answer.

Sati understands by meditating on Shiva that he has abandoned her. She becomes very sad but Shiva kept it a secret from her. Shiva narrates stories to her to keep her happy and tries to make her mind free from grief.

Shiva and Sati then reached Kailasa. Shiva went into deep meditation and Sati stayed in their home, feeling very sad. Shiva comes out of his meditation, Sati then greets him, and sits in front of him. He tells her many interesting stories and tries to make her happy. While doing this Shiva still keeps his promise.

Brahma says that some people tell the story of Sati and Shiva's separation, but in reality they are always together, like a word and its meaning, and cannot be separated. They only appear separated as part of their divine play. Their lives are a mystery and that they do whatever they choose.

Chapter Twenty Six

(HOW DAKSHA AND SHIVA BECAME ENEMIES)

This chapter tells the story of how a major argument caused a long-lasting feud between Daksha and Lord Shiva. It all happened at a big gathering at a holy place called Prayaga. Many wise people, gods, and sages came together for a special ceremony. They were having happy discussions and celebrating their faith.

Lord Shiva came with his wife Sati and his followers. When he arrived, everyone including Brahma, the creator of the universe, bowed to him to show their respect. They were all very happy to see him. Then, Daksha, a powerful leader, arrived. He was honored by many as well. He was proud and didn't fully understand Shiva's true nature. When Daksha entered, he was given a lot of respect, people sung his praises and bowed to him, however, Shiva did not bow to Daksha. Shiva remained seated and did not offer any respect to Daksha.

This made Daksha very angry. He thought Shiva was being disrespectful because he didn't bow down to him. Daksha said that Shiva is always surrounded by ghosts and does not follow any religious traditions. He called Shiva wicked, shameless, and said he was always lost in his love for his wife. He said that Shiva didn't belong at the gathering, and announced he was going to curse him.

Daksha said *"All the gods and wise people bow to me. But this person (Shiva), who is always with ghosts, is acting like a bad person. He doesn't respect me. He does not follow any rules and practices. He is always with spirits and is completely absorbed in his love. I am going to curse him."*

Daksha then declared that Shiva was an outcast and wouldn't get a share of the sacrifices with the gods, and that he should be seen as an outcaste.

Hearing Daksha's insults and curses, Shiva's follower, Nandin, got furious. Nandin angrily confronted Daksha, saying that Shiva was the reason why sacrifices succeed, and why any place was holy. Nandin said that Daksha had cursed Shiva thoughtlessly.

Nandin said *"You are a foolish and wicked person for cursing my lord Shiva. You have cursed the one who makes all sacrifices successful. You are ridiculing the one who creates and destroys the entire world."*

Daksha, still very angry, cursed Nandin and all of Shiva's followers in return.

Daksha said *"You and all of Shiva's followers are thrown out of all religious practices. You will be abandoned by everyone who follows the Vedic path. You all will be heretics, who drink wine and have matted hair, ashes, and bones as decorations."*

This made Nandin even more furious. He cursed Daksha and all of Daksha's followers. Nandin said they would become greedy, shameless beggars, who would not understand the real teachings of the Vedas.

Nandin said *"You and all of the brahmins who are against Shiva, you all only talk about the Vedas, but do not understand them. You will be full of greed, and desires. You will become beggars, performing sacrifices for low caste people. You will be poor, and fall to hell."* He also cursed Brahma, saying that he would forget his true devotion towards Shiva. He also said that Daksha would become goat-faced and always be focused on rituals, not on truth.

After all these curses, Brahma, who was the creator and also understood Shiva, scolded both Daksha and his followers. He tried to explain that they were wrong. Lord Shiva, after listening to Nandin, laughed and spoke calmly to him. Shiva taught Nandin not to get angry, saying that true knowledge was within, not outside.

Shiva said *"Do not get angry, Nandin. You cursed the Brahmins thinking I was cursed. The Vedas are the source of all knowledge and the self is in everything. Do not curse those who seek that knowledge. There is no one who cursed me here. I am the sacrifice, and all the parts of the sacrifice, and also outside the sacrifice. I am in everything, including you, him, and everyone else here. You cursed the Brahmins for no reason. Let go of your anger and understand the truth of everything."*

Nandin understood Shiva's teaching, he let go of his anger and decided to pursue true knowledge and wisdom. Shiva, having calmed everything down, returned to his home happily with his followers. But Daksha remained angry and left still seething with hatred. This event caused a rift between Daksha and Shiva, and Daksha began to hate everyone who worshipped Shiva.

Brahma concluded by saying this was the start of Daksha's hatred for Shiva and that he would continue the story.

Chapter Twenty Seven

(DAKSHA STARTS HIS SACRIFICE & MAKES A BIG MISTAKE)

This chapter tells about a grand sacrifice that Daksha organized, but also how it was flawed because of his hatred for Shiva. Daksha invited many wise sages, gods, and other important beings. He wanted to show off his power and greatness by having this huge ceremony. However, he made a big mistake by not inviting Lord Shiva and his wife, Sati.

Brahma explains that many great sages like Agastya, Kasyapa, and Bhrigu, along with many other powerful and noble beings, came to Daksha's sacrifice. They were all fooled by Shiva's Maya (illusion) into attending. Brahma, the creator, also came with his followers. Lord Vishnu, too, was invited and honored at the ceremony. Daksha arranged for big, beautiful homes for all the guests. He made sure everyone was treated well, except for Shiva and Sati.

Daksha intentionally did not invite Shiva because he thought Shiva was an outcast with no good family, who lived in cremation grounds with ghosts. He also did not invite his own daughter Sati because she was married to Shiva. Daksha believed Shiva was unworthy of attending and thought Sati was too because of her marriage.

In the middle of the ceremony, Dadhichi, a great devotee of Shiva, noticed that Shiva was not present. Dadhichi became very upset. He said that without Shiva, the sacrifice was incomplete and not right. He urged Daksha to invite Shiva immediately, saying that if Shiva accepted their invitation all the inauspicious things will become auspicious.

Dadhichi said *"Why isn't Shiva here? All the important gods and sages are here, but without Shiva, this sacrifice is incomplete. All good things happen because of him. We should invite Shiva immediately with all respect, along with Sati, to make this sacrifice perfect. Without him, this sacrifice is useless."* He continued and said that everything is purified when you think about Shiva and bring him here.

Daksha got very angry at Dadhichi's words. He bragged about how he had invited Vishnu, Brahma, and all the other gods. He said that the sacrifice was perfect without Shiva. Daksha insulted Shiva, calling him a homeless, fatherless, and motherless person who was always with ghosts. He stated that Shiva was too proud and not fit for the ceremony.

Daksha said *"Vishnu and Brahma are here, along with all the gods. This sacrifice is complete. Why do we need Shiva? I only married my daughter to him because Brahma persuaded me. He is a bad person, always with ghosts. He's not worthy of this sacred rite, and he was not invited by me."*

Dadhichi, angered by Daksha's arrogance and disrespect, said that Daksha's actions had turned the sacrifice into a "non-sacrifice", and that his destruction was near.

Dadhichi said *"This is not a real sacrifice without Shiva. Your destruction is close."*

Dadhichi then walked out of the ceremony, followed by other Shiva devotees. Daksha mockingly said that those who followed Shiva were fools and did not belong to Vedic circle.

Daksha said *"Good riddance. They are foolish and senseless. They are out of the Vedic circle. All of you, stay and make this sacrifice successful."*

Despite seeing the wise Dadhichi walk away and the others Shiva devotees leaving, the other celestial beings stayed to complete the sacrifice, blinded by Shiva's Maya. Brahma concluded by saying that he had explained how Daksha's sacrifice had been cursed and how he would now describe how it was destroyed.

Chapter Twenty Eight

(SATI'S JOURNEY TO THE SACRIFICE)

This chapter describes Sati's decision to go to her father Daksha's sacrifice, despite not being invited and against Shiva's advice. The story begins with Sati enjoying herself with her friends on a mountain. She notices the moon hurrying away with Rohini, and she asks her friend, Vijaya, where they are going. Vijaya finds out from the moon that they are heading to Daksha's big sacrifice. Vijaya then tells Sati about it.

Sati is surprised and hurt that her own father did not invite her. She wonders why her parents would forget her. She decides she needs to ask Shiva for the reason behind this. So she leaves her friends and goes to where Shiva is, in the middle of his assembly.

Sati comes to Shiva, and he welcomes her affectionately, taking her onto his lap.

Shiva said *"My dear wife, why have you come to my assembly looking so surprised? What is the reason?"*

Sati tells Shiva about the sacrifice, and asks why he does not want to go to her father's sacrifice. She asks why he doesn't want to go and wants him to go with her.

Sati said *"My lord, I have heard that my father is performing a big sacrifice. The gods and sages are gathering there, but it seems that you have no wish to attend it. Please tell me the reason for this. Friends should be with each other and enjoy. Please come with me to my father's sacrificial hall, just for me."*

Shiva, remembering Daksha's insults, politely refuses. He says that Daksha is his enemy, and that those who go uninvited to someone else's house are disrespected, which is worse than death.

Shiva said *"My dear Sati, your father is indeed your father but he is my enemy. Those who have not been invited should not go to someone's house otherwise they are greatly disrespected. So we, you and I, should not go to Daksha's sacrifice. I am telling you the truth. The words of enemies cause a lot of pain, but the words of relatives can be even more painful."*

Sati becomes angry, she says that her father did a bad thing by not inviting Shiva, who is the source of all the power of sacrifice. She wants to know the evil thoughts of her father and all the others who attended. She asks Shiva for permission to go to the sacrifice.

Sati said *"My lord, my father has insulted you by not inviting you to the sacrifice. I want to see the minds of those people who are against you. Please give me permission to go to my father's sacrifice."*

Shiva, knowing everything, but seeing that Sati really wanted to go, granted her permission.

Shiva said *"My goddess, if you really want to go and think it is the right thing to do, then you can go to your father's sacrifice, and I am giving you my permission."* He offers her his bull to ride and gives her all the royal things, like an umbrella, royal clothes and jewelry.

Sati, adorned in royal clothing, starts her journey to her father's home. Sixty thousand of Shiva's attendants go with her. They all sing songs praising Shiva and Sati, making the departure a very grand event. The three worlds were filled with happy sounds because of her departure.

Chapter Twenty Nine

(SATI SPEAKS OUT AT THE SACRIFICE)

This chapter details Sati's arrival at Daksha's sacrifice and her powerful speech where she confronts her father and the other attendees. When Sati arrives at the sacrifice, which was full of gods and sages, she sees the beautiful buildings and the large crowd. She gets off Nandin, the bull, and goes inside alone. Her mother and sisters welcome her respectfully, but Daksha doesn't even acknowledge her presence with respect or love, and others don't either because they are afraid of him.

Sati bows to her parents but is surprised at how coldly she is being treated. Then she notices that everyone has been given a share in the sacrifice, including Vishnu and the other gods, but there is no share for Shiva. This angers her greatly.

Sati said *"How can you not invite Shiva who is the source of all goodness? How can you have a sacrifice without Shiva, who is the sacrifice itself, the one performing the sacrifice, the benefit of the sacrifice, and the one who knows what sacrifice is? Any ritual without him is impure, but even just thinking about him makes it pure. Everything is identical to Shiva. Have you forgotten how great Shiva is?"* Sati was very furious, and she looked at Daksha and the others with anger.

She then scolds Vishnu, Brahma, and all the other gods and sages for attending the sacrifice without Shiva. She reminds them of times when Shiva was more powerful than them, and how they should know better.

Sati said to Vishnu *"O Vishnu, do you not know the real nature of Shiva? You have forgotten how many times Shiva has helped you. And yet you have the desire to attend a sacrifice where Shiva was not invited."*

Sati said to Brahma *"O Brahma, you had five faces before, but Shiva made you four-faced when you became arrogant. It is surprising you have forgotten this incident."*

Sati said to Indra *"O Indra, don't you know that Shiva once reduced your thunderbolt to ashes?"*

Sati also said to the sages *"O sages, have you forgotten how Shiva wandered as a beggar and when you cursed him, his Linga burned the entire universe?"*

Sati says that all of them have become foolish for not including Shiva, and that no one can understand Shiva through the Vedas alone.

After this fiery speech, everyone is silent. Daksha then turns to Sati with a cruel look and scolds her in return.

Daksha said *"My dear daughter, you can stay or leave. Why did you come here in the first place? Your husband Shiva is not a noble person. He is a king of goblins and ghosts and is not allowed to do the Vedic rites. That is why I did not invite him. I was foolish when I married you to him, and I know I was a sinner. Now just stop your anger, and take your share of the sacrifice."*

Sati, now very angry and in despair, thinks that she cannot return to Shiva after hearing such insults about him. She tells her father that anyone who insults Shiva goes to hell, and so does anyone who listens to those insults.

Sati said *"I will leave this body by entering fire. What is the value of life for me when I am forced to listen to these insults? Both the person who insults Shiva and the person who listens to such insults will go to hell for as long as the sun and the moon will last. Anyone who hurts Siva should have their tongue cut, if they are powerful, and if not they should close their ears and leave."*

She remembers Shiva's advice about going to her father's place uninvited and feels regret. She then continues her anger towards her father, and warns the other gods and sages about their foolishness. She says that Daksha will regret his hatred of Shiva, who is kind to everyone. She says that even just saying "Shi" and "Va" once is enough to cleanse any sin. She asks why Daksha is so wicked to hold ill feelings towards Shiva, who is holy, and that he is an enemy of Shiva.

She then states how it is a pity that they all think so bad of Shiva, who helps everyone and who is the source of liberation. She says that only her father considers Shiva unholy, all the other wise people like Brahma, Sanaka and the sages do not. She explains that Shiva lives with goblins and in the cremation grounds, but still, all the sages and gods keep the dust of his feet on their heads.

Sati concludes by stating that she does not want to be associated with Daksha anymore and that she will give up the body that she was given by him. She says that she has been called Dakshayani because of him and that it is distressing to her. She declares that all of them are evil for insulting Shiva and that Shiva will punish them for their actions. With these words Sati stops speaking after thinking of her beloved Shiva.

Chapter Thirty

(SATI GIVES UP HER BODY AND CHAOS ERUPTS)

This chapter describes how Sati ends her life at Daksha's sacrifice and the chaos that follows. After Sati finished her speech, she became quiet and remembered Shiva with great respect. She then sat on the ground, covered her body with her cloth, closed her eyes, and entered a deep yogic trance.

Sati controlled her breath, moving it through her body and finally to the center of her eyebrows. She was angry with Daksha and wanted to burn her body and only keep the pure air from her life through yogic means. While doing this, she thought only of Shiva's feet. Her body, now free of all sins, was burnt by the yogic fire, just as she had wished.

When everyone saw this, they cried out in horror. "Oh no! Shiva's beloved Sati has given up her life!" They wondered who was so wicked to have made her so angry. They called Daksha's act unholy. They said that because Daksha was so evil, he would become infamous in the whole world and go to hell for his actions.

When the attendants of Sati saw what had happened, they were overcome with anger. Sixty thousand of them, who had been waiting near the door, grabbed their weapons and started shouting, "Ha, Ha," and "Fie, Fie,". The gods and sages at the sacrifice became very afraid. The attendants all picked up their weapons and it was very loud. Some attendants were so sad they even cut off their own limbs, heads and faces with their sharp weapons. Twenty thousand of them also died with Sati.

The other attendants jumped up, ready to kill Daksha. Seeing them attack, the sage Bhrigu poured offerings into the sacrificial fire to create fire demons called Rbhus, to defend Daksha and stop the attacks of Sati's attendants.

The Rbhus started fighting the Shiva's attendants with fire weapons. The attendants were not as strong, so they were quickly killed or forced to flee. This was actually what Shiva had wanted to happen, and it all happened very quickly.

When the gods, sages, Indra and other deities saw what had happened, they were silent and afraid. They were all agitated and confused. They began to ponder on the effects of the chaos and destruction caused by the attendants of Shiva, also known as Pramathas. They also sought out Vishnu and other gods for help to stop any more trouble.

This is how the sacrifice of Daksha, who had become an enemy to Shiva, was destroyed and disrupted.

Chapter Thirty One

(THE VOICE FROM THE HEAVENS SPEAKS)

This chapter describes how a celestial voice speaks out at Daksha's sacrifice, after Sati's self-immolation. The voice scolds Daksha and warns everyone present about their mistakes.

As Daksha and the others were still reeling from Sati's death, a loud celestial voice suddenly spoke out. It addressed Daksha directly.

The Celestial Voice said *"O Daksha, you wicked and proud person, what have you done? Your foolish actions have caused great suffering! You should have listened to Dadhichi, the devotee of Shiva. If you had, everything would have been good. But you did not respect your own daughter Sati, even when she came to your house. You did not worship Sati and Shiva. You are a fool, even though you are Brahma's son. You are completely lost."*

The voice continues by explaining that Sati, who is the mother of the three worlds, is the one who removes all sins, she lives in Shiva's body, and she is the source of all good things. She should be worshipped always for all her goodness.

The voice said that Sati removes the fear of the world, grants all wishes, and removes all problems, she gives fame and wealth and both earthly pleasures and salvation. The voice declared that Sati is the creator, protector and destroyer of the universe. She is also the illusion of the universe, and she is the mother of everyone, from Vishnu and Brahma, to Indra and the sun. Sati gives the results of good actions, she is Shiva's power and she is the greatest of all.

The voice states that Daksha was foolish for not giving the correct share to Shiva, whose wife is Sati, and said Shiva is the one who is to be worshipped.

The voice declared that Shiva is the greatest lord and Vishnu, Brahma, and all the others serve him. The voice said that yogis meditate to see him and those who see Shiva get wealth, success and all their sacrifices are fulfilled. The voice declared that Shiva is the creator, the teacher, and the source of all good things.

The celestial voice said that because Daksha did not respect Shiva's power and because he is wicked, the sacrifice would be destroyed. The voice declared that those who do not worship those who should be worshipped will suffer. The voice explained that Sati is Shiva's power and that even the great serpent, Shesha, carries the dust of her feet on his head. The voice explained that Vishnu, Brahma, and all the gods and guardians only became powerful through worshiping Shiva and Sati's feet. The voice stated that Shiva is the father of the universe and Sati is the mother of the universe, and Daksha did not honor them.

The voice then told Daksha that because he did not please Shiva and Sati, bad things had happened to him, and that if he thought he could be successful without worshipping Shiva, his pride would be destroyed.

The Celestial Voice continued *"I don't see any of these gods who will help you, because you are against the Lord. If any of the gods try to help you, they will be destroyed. Your sacrifice will be destroyed. Anyone who helps you will also be destroyed, immediately."*

The voice cursed all the gods for their inaction and for their misdeed. The voice ordered all the gods, sages, Nagas and others to leave the sacrifice or be destroyed immediately and told Brahma and Vishnu to get away from the sacrifice quickly or they would also die.

After saying all of this, the celestial voice stopped speaking. Vishnu and the other gods and sages were all very surprised and confused by what they had heard.

Chapter Thirty Two

(VIRABHADRA IS BORN AND SHIVA'S ORDERS)

This chapter describes the birth of Virabhadra and Shiva's instructions to him to destroy Daksha's sacrifice. Narada asks Brahma what happened after the celestial voice spoke, and what happened to Shiva's defeated attendants.

Brahma explains that after the voice from the sky, all the gods and other beings were surprised and silent. The Shiva's attendants, who had been defeated by Bhrigu's mantras, ran to Shiva for help. They bowed to Shiva and told him everything that had happened at Daksha's sacrifice.

The Ganas (Shiva's Attendants) said *"Oh lord, save us. Daksha disrespected Sati and the gods did not help. He did not give you a share in the sacrifice and insulted you. Sati was angry and burned herself. Thousands of our fellow attendants killed themselves out of shame. We tried to stop them, but Bhrigu pushed us back using his power. We are now afraid and seek your help. Please help us."*

When Shiva heard all of this he remembered Narada to understand everything in detail. Narada, who had a divine vision, appeared and bowed to Shiva. Shiva asked Narada about what had happened and Narada told Shiva about what he had seen. Shiva became very angry when he heard about what had happened at Daksha's sacrifice.

In his fury, Shiva plucked a lock of his matted hair and struck it against a mountain. The hair split in two, creating a loud noise like the end of the world. From one half, Virabhadra, a powerful warrior with two thousand hands, appeared. He was huge and terrifying. From Shiva's angry breath, many fevers and diseases were created. From the other half, Mahakali, a terrible goddess surrounded by goblins, was born.

Virabhadra bowed to Shiva and asked what he should do.

Virabhadra said *"Oh, Rudra, what do you want me to do? Shall I dry up the oceans? Shall I turn the mountains into dust? Shall I destroy the universe? Thanks to your blessing, nothing is impossible for me. I will do whatever you ask of me. With your favour even the most worthless people cross over difficult situations. Send me on any errand and I will do it. Even a blade of grass sent by you will achieve great tasks. With your blessing, I am qualified in this task, for without it none can be powerful."*

Shiva was pleased with Virabhadra. He blessed him and then gave him instructions. Lord Shiva said *"Oh Virabhadra, listen carefully. Daksha, that wicked son of Brahma, has arranged a sacrifice. He is my enemy. He is very foolish and arrogant. Destroy the sacrifice completely and come back to me quickly. If you see gods, Gandharvas, Yakshas, or others, turn them to ash. If Vishnu, Brahma, Indra, or Yama try to stop you, fight them too. Anyone who defied Dadhichi and stayed at the sacrifice should be burned. Even if they praise you, burn them anyway. After burning Daksha and all the others at the sacrifice, come back to me quickly."*

After giving these instructions, Shiva, still angry, stopped speaking.

Chapter Thirty Three

(VIRABHADRA'S MARCH TO THE SACRIFICE)

This chapter describes Virabhadra's grand march towards Daksha's sacrifice, following Shiva's orders. After receiving Shiva's instructions, Virabhadra became very happy and bowed to Shiva with great respect. He then immediately set off towards the place of the sacrifice.

Shiva sent countless of his Ganas (attendants), who were as powerful as the fire of destruction, to accompany Virabhadra. These attendants, full of energy and joy, went both in front of and behind Virabhadra. They looked like Shiva, with the same clothes, features, and decorations. Virabhadra rode in a chariot pulled by ten thousand strong lions. His bodyguards included many lions, tigers, crocodiles, and elephants. When Virabhadra left for Daksha's sacrifice, flowers fell from the divine Kalpa tree. The Ganas praised Virabhadra and were very excited.

Mahakali, along with nine other Durgas: Kali, Katyayani, Ishani, Chamunda, Mundamardini, Bhadrakali, Bhadra, Tvarita and Vaishnavi, also went ahead to destroy Daksha. They were accompanied by many goblins. They were eager to carry out Shiva's command. Many powerful beings accompanied them, including Dakinis, Sakinis, Bhutas, Pramathas, Guhyakas, Kusmandas, Parpatas, Gatakas, Brahma-Rakshasas, Bhairavas, and Kshetrapalas. They all hurried to destroy Daksha's sacrifice.

The Yoginis also went to destroy the sacrifice. Brahma then describes the large numbers of Ganas who were part of the procession of Virabhadra. The chief Ganas, Sankukarpa, Kekaraksha, Vikrita, Visakha, Pariyatraka, Sarvankaka, Vikritanana, Jvalakesa, Dhiman, Dudrabha, Kapalisa, Sandaraka, Kotikundha, Vistambha, Sannada, Pippala, Avesana, Candratapana, Mahavesa, Kundi, Pavataka, Kala, Kalaka, Mahakala, Agnikrit, Agnimukha,

Adityamurdha, Ghanavaha, Sannaha, Kumuda, Amogha, Kokila, Kashtagudha, Sukesi, Vrishabha, Sumantraka, Kakapadodara, Santanaka, Mahabala, Pungava, Madhupinga, Purnabhadra, Caturvaktra, Virupaksha, Talaketu, Shatashya, Panchashya, Samvartaka, Kulisa, Svayamprabhu, Lokantaka, Diptatma, Daityantaka, Bhringiriti, Devadevapriya, Ashani, and Bhalaka, each with their own huge armies and numbers.

Virabhadra, followed by these countless attendants, and accompanied by goblins and three crores canine species born of Shiva's hair, moved quickly towards Daksha's sacrifice. Trumpets, drums, conchs, and horns all sounded loudly, and many instruments played music during their march. As they moved forward, many good omens appeared, indicating their success.

Chapter Thirty Four

(BAD OMENS AT DAKSHA'S SACRIFICE)

This chapter describes the terrible omens that appeared at Daksha's sacrifice as Virabhadra and his army approached. As Virabhadra and his forces set off, Daksha and the gods began to see many bad signs.

Three major bad omens appeared to show that Daksha's sacrifice would be destroyed. Daksha's left eye, arm and thigh twitched and throbbed constantly, which was a very bad sign. There was an earthquake, and the stars could be seen in the middle of the day. The sky became dirty and dark, and the sun appeared terrifying with thousands of circles around it. Stars that looked like fire or lightning fell down from the sky.

Thousands of vultures flew above, touching Daksha's head and making shadows on the sacrificial area. Jackals howled near the sacrifice, and falling meteors looked like white scorpions. Strong winds blew dust everywhere, and locusts and moths were caught up in whirlwinds. The new sacrificial platform that Daksha had made was also destroyed by the wind.

Even more strangely, Daksha and others started vomiting blood, pieces of flesh, and bones very frequently. They became weak and shaky, and felt like they had been cut by sharp weapons. Their eyes changed strangely; sometimes they looked like dying lotuses, sometimes like forest flowers with dew, sometimes like lotuses at night and sometimes like kumuda flowers in the morning. The gods seemed to be showering blood, and everywhere was dark with a strange terrifying light.

All of these bad omens scared the gods and others, including Vishnu. They cried, "We are doomed," and then they fell unconscious to the ground like trees falling into a river. They lay there still, like dead snakes, and sometimes they bounced like balls. They cried out like birds, and their voices all mixed together. Everyone's power was taken away, and they all rolled around like tortoises bumping into each other.

Then, a voice from the sky spoke out to Daksha and the gods.

The Ethereal Voice said *"You evil and foolish Daksha, your life is now worthless! Great suffering from Shiva will come to you. And you foolish gods and others who are crying, you will also face terrible misery!"*

Chapter Thirty Five

(VISHNU'S WARNING)

This chapter describes Daksha pleading with Vishnu for help and Vishnu's explanation about the power of Shiva and the hopelessness of their situation. Daksha, seeing the bad omens, goes to Vishnu for protection.

Daksha said *"Oh Hari, Vishnu, lord of the gods, you are the friend of the poor and full of mercy. Please protect me and my sacrifice. You are the one who protects sacrifices. Oh Lord, please have mercy, and do not let my sacrifice be destroyed."*

Daksha falls at Vishnu's feet out of fear. Vishnu picks him up, and after remembering Shiva, Vishnu speaks to Daksha.

Vishnu said *"Listen Daksha, I will tell you the truth. You have insulted Shiva, who is the greatest lord of all, because you did not understand him. Insulting Shiva makes everything useless and causes many problems. When those who are supposed to be worshipped are not respected, and when those who do not deserve respect are honored, poverty, death, and fear will come. Shiva must always be respected. Because Shiva has been disrespected here, we are all in great trouble. Even though we are lords, we cannot do anything now because of your mistakes."*

When Daksha heard this, he became very quiet and his face turned pale. At that moment, Virabhadra arrived at the sacrifice with his army, as Shiva had ordered. The attendants came from everywhere, roaring like lions. The earth shook, and the oceans and mountains were disturbed.

Daksha, now terrified, fell at Vishnu's feet again, along with his wife.

Daksha said *"Oh Vishnu, I started this sacrifice because I believed in you. You are the protector of good actions and sacrifices. Please protect my sacrifice here, because you are the lord of all"*

Vishnu, though knowing that Daksha hated Shiva, tries to reason with him.

Vishnu said *"Daksha, I will try to protect your sacrifice, as I have promised to protect Dharma. However, you have ignored the truth. You have forgotten what happened at Naimisha. No one can save you from Shiva's anger. Anyone who tries to protect you, a wicked person, will not be liked. You need to know that the actions that give the best results are the ones done with love of God, and only Shiva can give the result of good actions."*

Vishnu explained that those who only depend on knowledge and not devotion to God will fall to hell and that those who only rely on actions will be stuck in a cycle of birth and death. Vishnu explains that Virabhadra has come to destroy them and that nothing is impossible for him.

Vishnu continued *"I know that this lord will only be satisfied after burning us all. Because of my mistake in going against Shiva, I will also have to face the pain, along with you. I have no power to stop this. There can be no happiness to the enemies of Shiva. My discus, Sudarshana, will not hurt Virabhadra, because my discus only hurts non-devotees of Shiva. If Virabhadra was not here, this discus would have killed us and gone back to Shiva. This discus has stayed with me only because it is compassionate, and it won't stay with me for long."*

Vishnu stated that even if they worship Virabhadra, it will not help. He said that everyone's destruction is near, and there is no one who can save them from Shiva's anger. He also says that they will suffer in hell at the hands of Yama. He says he was wrong not to leave earlier. He knows that even if they try to run, Virabhadra will find them. Vishnu says that even the smallest of Shiva's attendants is very powerful. Vishnu mentioned that at Kashi Kalabhairava had plucked off one of Brahma's heads with his fingernail.

After saying this, Vishnu sat down with a fearful expression. At the same time, they saw Virabhadra's vast army arriving at the sacrifice.

Chapter Thirty Six

(THE ROUT OF THE GODS: VIRABHADRA'S FURY)

This chapter of the Shiva Purana describes the intense battle that unfolds after Daksha's yagna (fire sacrifice) is disrupted. Initially, Indra, mocking Vishnu's advice, rallies the gods to fight Virabhadra and Shiva's ganas (attendants). The gods, mounted on their animals, and the Yakshas, Caranas, and Guhyakas get ready to fight. Daksha encourages them, saying his sacrifice depends on their strength.

The battle starts with fierce fighting between the gods and the ganas. Sharp weapons and iron clubs clash, drums sound, and conchs are blown. Bhrigu's incantations and rituals push back Shiva's attendants, making them suffer losses. This enrages Virabhadra who commands his forces and leads the attack. He sends forth attendants on bulls and attacks with his trident, defeating the gods. The gods are routed and flee, leaving only the guardians of the directions, Indra and others.

These remaining gods turn to their teacher, Brihaspati, for help. Brihaspati reminds them of Vishnu's earlier warning and explains that Shiva is beyond the understanding of the Vedas, rituals, or worldly actions. He says that only devotion can help in understanding and knowing Shiva. He also points out their foolishness in fighting in this yagna. He tells them that the attendants of Rudra have come to stop the sacrifice and they will succeed because there is no preventing it.

Virabhadra then approaches Indra and the other remaining gods and threatens to dismember them. He showers them with arrows causing the remaining gods, including the guardians of the directions, to flee.

The sages at the sacrificial site are terrified. They appeal to Vishnu for protection. They call Vishnu as the protector of sacrifice and urge him to save Daksha's yagna. Vishnu, now armed, comes to fight Virabhadra.

Virabhadra questions Vishnu on why he defied Shiva's affirmation. They meet like death and sin, lion and elephant. Virabhadra criticizes Vishnu for supporting Daksha and challenges him to a fight.

Vishnu explains that he is a servant of Shiva and came only to fulfil the request of Daksha. He adds that he will fight Virabhadra and show his prowess. Hearing this, Virabhadra is pleased that Vishnu is devoted to Shiva. Virabhadra then reveals that he was merely testing Vishnu. He explains that Shiva and Vishnu are one and that all are the servants of Shiva and do the bidding of Shiva. He finally asks Vishnu to fight him. Vishnu agrees and tells Virabhadra to hit him with arrows so he can return to his hermitage. Both get ready to fight.

Chapter Thirty Seven

(THE DESTRUCTION OF DAKSHA'S SACRIFICE)

This chapter details the fierce battle and the complete annihilation of Daksha's sacrifice by Virabhadra and his ganas. The chapter begins with Virabhadra, meditating on Shiva, preparing for battle with Vishnu and roaring like a lion. Vishnu responds by blowing his conch, which brings back the fleeing gods to the battlefield. The gods, led by Indra, charge into battle again, fighting with Shiva's ganas.

Fierce battles break out: Indra fights Nandin, the fire-god battles Asman, and Kubera clashes with Kusmandapati. These battles are intense, with both sides dealing heavy blows. The ganas inflict more significant damage to gods. The chief ganas attack various gods - Mahaloka fights Yama, Chanda mortifies Nairrta, Munda battles Varuna, and Bhrngi fights the wind god. The Yoginis and Kali drink the blood of leading gods, while Ksetrapala does the same.

Vishnu then enters the fray, hurling his discus, which seems to scorch the directions. Ksetrapala bravely catches it, but Vishnu retrieves it by forcing him to spit it out. Enraged, Vishnu fights fiercely, with weapons and power but is met with equally strong forces. Virabhadra joins the battle against Vishnu, and a fierce fight ensues. Vishnu creates soldiers from his own body, but Virabhadra, remembering Shiva, destroys them with his trident. Virabhadra then strikes Vishnu in the chest, causing him to fall unconscious. Vishnu revives, enraged. He attempts to strike with his discus but, by Shiva's power, the discus becomes immobilized in his hand. Vishnu becomes stunned. He then recovers from his state of unconsciousness and tries to attack with his bow. Virabhadra breaks the bow into three pieces with three arrows.

Realizing the ganas are invincible, Vishnu withdraws, knowing all this is a consequence of Sati's self-immolation. He goes back to his world along with other gods and sages. When they left, the remaining participants of the yagna were defeated by the ganas. The yagna itself, scared, flees in the form of a deer, which Virabhadra beheads.

Virabhadra then humiliates the remaining participants. He kicks prominent sages like Prajapati, Dharma, Kashyapa, Angiras, and Krsasva on their heads. He mutilates Saraswati's and Aditi's noses. He throws other gods to the ground. He doesn't stop in his fury. Virabhadra next attacks Bhrigu, while Manibhadra kicks him on the chest and plucks off his moustaches. Chanda plucks out the teeth of Pushan, and Nandin pulls out Bhaga's eyes because he winked at Daksha when cursing Shiva. The ganas defile the sacrificial fire and make the yagna impure.

Finally, Virabhadra finds Daksha hiding behind the altar and drags him out. He tries to behead him, but because of Daksha's yogic power, it's not possible with a sword. He then kicks Daksha in the chest and rips off his head with his hand, throwing it into the sacrificial fire.

Virabhadra then burns Daksha, along with all that remained, in the fire. He laughs a boisterous laugh that echoes throughout the three worlds. After fulfilling his duty, he goes to Kailasa. Shiva, pleased with Virabhadra, makes him the head of his ganas.

Chapter Thirty Eight

(THE STORY OF DADHICHI'S POWER AND VISHNU'S PREDICAMENT)

This chapter explains why Vishnu participated in Daksha's yagna, despite knowing of Shiva's power, and why he fought against Shiva's ganas. Narada asks Brahma why Vishnu, knowing Shiva's strength, would go to Daksha's sacrifice and fight with Shiva's attendants. Brahma explains that Vishnu's actions were influenced by a curse from Sage Dadhichi.

Brahma recounts the story of a dispute between King Ksuva and Sage Dadhichi, who were friends. Dadhichi, a devotee of Shiva, claimed Brahmins are superior. Ksuva, proud of his kingship, argued that kings are greater, as they embody the eight guardians of the world and are divine. This angered Dadhichi, who struck Ksuva on the head. In return, Ksuva hit Dadhichi with a thunderbolt.

Dadhichi, remembering his ancestor Sukra, was saved by his powers. Sukra then taught Dadhichi the powerful Mahamrityunjaya mantra, a mantra dedicated to Shiva which can conquer death. Sukra explained that the three-eyed lord Shiva is the essence of everything. He instructed Dadhichi to worship Shiva with devotion through rituals and meditation. He mentions that those who meditate in presence of Siva have no fear of death. He then describes the form of Lord Shiva that must be meditated upon.

Dadhichi, following Sukra's instructions, went to the forest and performed severe penance and repeated the mantra for a long time. Pleased, Shiva appeared before him and granted him three boons: adamantine bones (bones as strong as diamonds), invincibility, and freedom from distress. Now empowered, Dadhichi returned and kicked

Ksuva on the head with the sole of his foot. Ksuva, in turn, tried to hit Dadhichi with his thunderbolt but it had no effect. Ksuva was defeated.

Humiliated, Ksuva sought help from Vishnu. Vishnu, pleased with Ksuva's devotion, appeared to him. Ksuva told Vishnu how Dadhichi had humiliated him and that Dadhichi's power was due to Shiva. Vishnu recognized Shiva's strength. Vishnu then told Ksuva that Shiva devotees are fearless, and that he will be cursed along with the other gods and trouble will arise due to it. He reveals that he is destined to be destroyed at Daksha's yagna by Shiva's ganas but will rise again. Vishnu promised to help Ksuva but acknowledged the superiority of Shiva and the invincibility of his devotees. Vishnu also added that Daksha's yagna would not be completed. He promised Ksuva that he would help him defeat Dadhichi.

This explains that Vishnu, aware of Shiva's power, still went to Daksha's sacrifice to help Ksuva and because of the curse. This also shows the power of devotion to Lord Shiva and the futility of confronting those protected by Shiva.

Chapter Thirty Nine

(THE SHOWDOWN BETWEEN VISHNU AND DADHICHI)

This chapter describes the intense fight between Vishnu and Sage Dadhichi, showing the power of Dadhichi due to his devotion to Shiva. Brahma narrates that Vishnu, wanting to help Ksuva, disguised himself as a Brahmin and visited Dadhichi's hermitage.

Vishnu, in disguise, asked Dadhichi for a favor. Dadhichi, a devoted follower of Shiva, immediately recognized Vishnu's true identity. He stated that due to Shiva's grace, he knows the past, present, and future and everything is clear to him. He then revealed that he knew Vishnu was acting on behalf of Ksuva and asked him to drop the disguise and show his real form and remember Shiva. He also stated that since his mind is always on Shiva he never lies and has no fear of anyone.

Vishnu then requested that Dadhichi just say he was afraid once, for the sake of Vishnu and Ksuva. Dadhichi, unafraid, laughed and replied that he had no fear due to the power of Shiva. This made Vishnu angry. Vishnu revealed himself and stood ready to attack with his discus. The discus, however, became useless before Dadhichi, due to the power of Shiva. Dadhichi then told Vishnu that the discus, Sudarshana, was Shiva's discus and so it can't kill him. He challenged Vishnu to hurl all his weapons.

Vishnu, thinking Dadhichi was an ordinary man, hurled all his weapons. The gods, supporting Vishnu, also attacked Dadhichi. Dadhichi, remembering Shiva, took a fistful of Kusha grass and threw it at the gods. The Kusha grass transformed into tridents, due to Shiva's grace, which threatened to burn the gods. The gods' weapons bowed before it and the gods fled, leaving only Vishnu.

Vishnu then created millions of beings like himself and sent them to fight Dadhichi. However, Dadhichi, burning with Shiva's power, defeated all of them. Vishnu then used his powers of illusion and showed Dadhichi a vision in which thousands of gods and creatures existed in his body. Dadhichi, however, saw through Vishnu's illusion. He said that he could also show the universe in his own body to Vishnu. He then revealed the universe to Vishnu within him which also included Brahma and Rudra.

Dadhichi, fearless, asked Vishnu to abandon his tricks and fight properly. Seeing Dadhichi infused with Shiva's brilliance, Vishnu became angry again. The gods also returned to support Vishnu. At this moment, Ksuva stopped Vishnu and the gods from fighting further. Ksuva, upset with Vishnu's defeat, approached Dadhichi and requested that Dadhichi bless him and Vishnu.

Dadhichi, angered seeing Vishnu and other gods, cursed Vishnu and the gods to be burnt by Rudra's anger. He then declared that brahmins should be respected by everyone. He then returned to his hermitage. Ksuva also returned to his palace, Vishnu to his abode, and other gods to their respective places.

The place where this encounter happened became a sacred place called Sthaneshvara. It is said that pilgrims visiting this place will be freed and reach Sayujya with Shiva.

The chapter concludes that those who read or listen to the story of this battle will not face premature death, and if they go to battle, they will come out victorious. This chapter emphasizes the power of devotion to Shiva.

Chapter Forty

(THE JOURNEY TO KAILASA AND THE VISION OF SHIVA)

This chapter describes the journey of Brahma, Vishnu, the gods, and the sages to Mount Kailasa to seek forgiveness from Shiva, after the destruction of Daksha's sacrifice.

Narada asks Brahma about what happened after Virabhadra returned to Kailasa. Brahma says that after being defeated by Shiva's forces, the gods and sages came to him for help. Brahma was pained by the suffering of Daksha and sought a way to restore him to life and complete the sacrifice.

He sought guidance from Vishnu. Accompanied by the gods and sages, Brahma went to Vishnu's abode and explained their misery. Vishnu, remembering Shiva, said that the gods had offended Shiva by taking his share of the sacrifice. He advised them to propitiate Shiva with a pure mind and ask for forgiveness. Vishnu also stated that Shiva had been hurt by Daksha's harsh words. He also added that he too had offended Shiva and will come with them to seek forgiveness. He says no one knows the full power of Shiva.

Following Vishnu's command, Brahma, Vishnu, the gods, and the sages went to Kailasa, Shiva's auspicious abode. Kailasa is a beautiful, divine mountain with peaks full of gems, various trees and creepers, and celestial beings. The river Ganga, flowing from where Sati's body had been, made the place holy. The group saw Alaka, Kubera's beautiful city, and Saugandhika, a divine park. They also saw the rivers Nanda and Alakananda where celestial damsels bathed.

Beyond Alaka and the park, they saw a huge fig tree where Shiva practiced yoga. It was a divine place, resorted to by other yogis. Beneath this tree, Vishnu and the others saw Shiva sitting calmly. Shiva was surrounded by Brahma's sons, Siddhas, Kubera, and his attendants.

Shiva had a divine form, loved by all, and had ashes smeared on his body. He was seated on Kusa grass, his left leg placed on his right thigh. A Rudraksha garland hung from his wrist and he held his hand in the Tarka mudra (a hand gesture).

Upon seeing Shiva, Vishnu and the gods humbly bowed with joined palms. Shiva stood up and bowed to Vishnu. Vishnu and the other gods bowed at Shiva's feet. Vishnu and others offered praises to Lord Shiva, who was revered by gods, Siddhas, Ganas, and sages.

Chapter Forty One

(PRAISING SHIVA: A PLEA FOR FORGIVENESS)

This chapter describes the heartfelt praise and plea for forgiveness offered to Lord Shiva by Vishnu, Brahma, and other gods.

The gods, led by Vishnu, address Shiva, acknowledging him as the supreme being, both Siva and Brahman, due to his grace. They state that Shiva has deluded them with his illusion which deceives all beings. They recognize Shiva as the ultimate reality, beyond the universe, and the one who creates, sustains, and destroys everything.

They admit that Shiva created the sacrifice through Daksha for the fulfillment of the Vedas. They acknowledge that all Vedic rituals and their limits culminate in Shiva. The gods realize that good actions lead to happiness, while bad actions lead to suffering, and that Shiva is the ultimate bestower of the results. They condemn those who are overly focused on rituals, and who are jealous and cause harm to others.

The gods beseech Shiva not to destroy them and show mercy. They offer praises to Shiva as the calm, supreme soul, with matted hair, and great power. They say that he is the creator of the creators, the sustainer and the very universe itself, greater than nature and the supreme being. They hail him as the blue-necked one, the cause of bliss in the universe. They recognize him in the form of Omkara, Vashatkara, the initiator of actions, and the receiver of offerings. They wonder why Shiva would disrupt the yagna as he is the benefactor of brahmins and destroyer of sacrifices. They acknowledge Shiva as the protector of virtue, brahmins, and cows, the shelter for all beings.

The gods then praise Shiva in his various forms, as light, liquid, fragrant earth, fire, wind, ether, moon, sun, the detached performer of action, Ugra, Bhima, controller of beings, the all pervasive soul and destroyer of distress. They hail him as the supreme being of all objects, as the cause of intellect, omniformed, plentiful, as Nila, Nilarudra, Kadrudra, and Pracetas. They praise him as the greatest, the destroyer of enemies of the gods. They bow to him as Tara, Sutara, Taruna, and brilliant. They praise Shiva as the beneficent one to gods, the great soul, the dark necked one, the golden one, and one who engages in terrible deeds.

They praise him as the one with ashes on his body, with Rudraksha beads, with various weapons, the slayer of Daityas and Danavas, and in the form of Vama, Aghora, Tatpurusa, and Isana. They praise him as the fierce destroyer of evil and the protector of the good. They revere Shiva as the one who swallowed the poison, Kalakuta. They praise him as Vira, Virabhadra, and Srikantha. They hail him as the greatest of the great, all-pervading, omniformed, Visnukalatra, Visnukshetra, and Bhairava. They praise him as Mrityunjaya and the cause of all causes. They acknowledge that the entire universe is pervaded by Shiva's splendour and he is the unchanging consciousness, bliss and light. They state that all the gods are born from him. They say that he is Astamurti as he holds everything by dividing his cosmic body into eight.

The gods say that it is Shiva's power that causes wind to blow, fire to blaze, sun to shine, and death to run everywhere. They beg Shiva, the ocean of mercy, to save them, as they are doomed without his grace. They remind Shiva that he has always protected them from miseries and ask him to do so now. They also beg him to revive Daksha's yagna. The gods ask Shiva to restore Bhaga's sight, bring Daksha back to life, regrow Pushan's teeth and Bhrigu's mustaches. They request Shiva to heal the mutilated bodies of the gods and others. They promise that Shiva will receive his due share in the yagna which will be officiated by Vasistha.

Finally, Vishnu, along with Brahma, prostrate before Shiva, begging for his forgiveness. This chapter emphasizes the supreme power of Lord Shiva, and the gods recognize their error, and seek forgiveness.

Chapter Forty Two

(DAKSHA'S MISERY ENDS: A NEW BEGINNING)

This chapter describes how Lord Shiva, pleased with the prayers and pleas for forgiveness from the gods, restores Daksha, the gods, and the disrupted sacrifice.

Brahma narrates that Shiva was delighted by the conciliatory words of Vishnu, Brahma, and the sages. He consoles them with a smile and explains that he has always borne their anger. He says he doesn't consider the mistakes of his children as sins. He states that he only punished those who were deluded by his illusion. He clarifies that he did not destroy Daksha's yagna, and that when one hates another, it ultimately harms the hater. He says he would never inflict pain on others.

Shiva then declares the consequences and restorations of the yagna. He announces that Daksha's head will be replaced with that of a goat. Bhaga will receive his share in the sacrifice with the sun. Pushan's teeth, broken for gripping the offerings, will remain broken. Bhrigu, who opposed Shiva, will have a goat's beard. He added that the gods who tried to uproot him will get their original bodies. He says that the Adhvaryu priests will be carried by the Ashwins and the hands of Pushan.

Vishnu and the other gods were pleased with Shiva's words. At their request, Shiva went to Kanakhala at the sacrificial altar. There he observed the destruction caused by Virabhadra to the yagna and the sages. He called Virabhadra and questioned him about the destruction and asked him to bring Daksha.

Virabhadra brought Daksha's headless body and laid it before Shiva. Shiva then asked Virabhadra about Daksha's head. When Virabhadra informed him that it was consigned to fire, Shiva ordered the gods to proceed. Following Shiva's instructions, Vishnu and other gods quickly fixed the head of a goat onto Daksha's body and told Bhrigu about it.

When the head was attached, Daksha was restored to life and woke up from a deep sleep. He was happy to see Shiva, who was merciful to him. Daksha's heart, which was previously filled with hatred for Shiva, became pure. However, he was emotionally disturbed and anxious for his deceased daughter. After regaining composure, a ashamed Daksha bowed and praised Shiva as the supreme being, the bestower of boons, and the sole kin of the universe.

He confessed his foolishness in not understanding Shiva's true nature. He realized that Shiva was served by Vishnu, Brahma, and others and could only be understood through the Vedas. He praised Shiva as the Kalpa tree to the good and punisher of the wicked. He asked forgiveness for his harsh words and for causing pain to the gods. He acknowledged Shiva as the helper of the distressed and the one who is satisfied with his own actions.

After Daksha, Vishnu praised Shiva with tears in his eyes. He hailed Shiva as the great Brahman and supreme soul. He said that Daksha was his devotee but also acknowledged Daksha's offense. Vishnu asked Shiva to forgive Daksha. He also confessed his own mistake in fighting with Virabhadra. Vishnu then proclaimed his servanthood to Shiva and sought his protection.

Brahma then praised Shiva and thanked him for blessing Daksha with a body. He asked Shiva to restore the sacrifice and remove all curses.

Finally, Indra and other gods, and the lower ranks of gods, also praised Shiva. This chapter shows Shiva's immense mercy and his ability to forgive those who seek his grace and acknowledges his position as supreme deity. It also demonstrates the importance of seeking forgiveness and rectifying one's mistakes.

Chapter Forty Three

(SHIVA'S WISDOM AND THE COMPLETION OF DAKSHA'S SACRIFICE)

This chapter tells the story of how Lord Shiva, after being angry and destroying Daksha's sacrifice, explains some important spiritual truths and then helps Daksha complete his sacrifice successfully.

First, Lord Shiva is happy with the praise from Vishnu, Brahma, and others. He tells Daksha that although he is the supreme lord, he always helps his devotees. He says there are four types of people who worship him: those in trouble, those curious about him, those seeking wealth and those with wisdom. Of these, the wise are closest to him and he considers them to be a part of himself. He also explains that only those who study the Vedas and understand the true knowledge of the self will know him. People who simply do rituals won't be able to find him, he tells Daksha, this is why he was angry with Daksha's ritual-only sacrifice.

Shiva then explains that rituals are okay but one must also have true knowledge of god and see him as the great lord. He reveals a deep truth: Brahma, Vishnu, and Shiva are the main forces behind the universe, but Shiva is the soul, the witness to all that happens and has no qualities. It is Shiva that enters his illusion and appears as Brahma (creator), Vishnu (sustainer), and Shiva (destroyer). He explains that wise followers do not feel separate from living beings or see any difference in the trinity. Those who see a difference, will go to hell. Devotion to any of the three, leads to knowledge of all, and finally salvation, he says. Shiva makes it very clear that hating one of the Trinity results in curses and no salvation.

Hearing all this, Daksha and everyone else realizes the truth about Shiva and is filled with devotion. Lord Shiva is pleased, grants everyone boons, and allows Daksha to complete the sacrifice. Daksha gives Shiva the largest share, other gods their shares, and gives gifts to Brahmins, earning Shiva's blessing. Everyone is happy now, and Daksha's sacrifice is completed successfully by Shiva's grace. The sages then leave with happy hearts, singing the glory of Lord Shiva. Vishnu and Brahma also return to their abodes.

Shiva, honored by Daksha, returns to his home, Kailasa, with his followers. He remembers his wife, Sati, and tells her story. The chapter explains that even Lord Shiva does things that seem like human emotions to teach people, but he is beyond delusion or sorrow. He is difficult to understand, even for Vishnu and Brahma, but easy for devotees who are devoted to him.

Finally, it is mentioned that Sati, who gave up her life earlier, took birth as the daughter of Himavat and Mena and through penance, she again wooed Shiva as her husband and became half his body. Listening to this story brings worldly happiness and salvation. Anyone who reads or teaches this story will reach the greatest spiritual goal after their life and achieve both happiness and salvation.